Barrington Renford Patterson is [...] Mixed Martial Arts fighter. The [...] Ring' is well-known to cage-fi[...] notorious as one of Britain's 'Hard Men' – as testified by a full episode of the TV series *Danny Dyer's Deadliest Men*. The former football hooligan from the Birmingham Zulus firm also cuts a powerful figure in clubland, with a hard-earned reputation gained by running some of the roughest doors in the Midlands.

Cass Pennant is the author of eight books on football hooliganism, five of which have been UK Top 10 best-sellers. His bestselling autobiography (*Cass*) was published by John Blake and made into a critically acclaimed feature film. As an authority on hooligan and gang culture, he has advised on TV and film projects including Guy Ritchie's *Snatch*, Alan Clarke's *The Firm*, Lexi Alexander's *Green Street*, ITV's *Bouncers* series and Bravo's *The Real Football Factories* – where he was introduced to Barrington.

ONE-EYED BAZ

ONE-EYED BAZ

**THE STORY OF BARRINGTON
'ZULU' PATTERSON, ONE OF
BRITAIN'S DEADLIEST MEN**

BARRINGTON PATTERSON
WITH CASS PENNANT

JOHN BLAKE

Published by John Blake Publishing Ltd,
3 Bramber Court, 2 Bramber Road,
London W14 9PB, England

www.johnblakebooks.com

www.facebook.com/johnblakebooks ▪

twitter.com/jblakebooks ▪

First published in paperback in 2013

ISBN: 978-1-84358-811-5

British Library Cataloguing-in-Publication Data:

A catalogue record for this book is available from the British Library.

Design by www.envydesign.co.uk

Printed in Great Britain by CPI Group (UK) Ltd

Papers used by John Blake Publishing are natural, recyclable products made
from wood grown in sustainable forests. The manufacturing processes
conform to the environmental regulations of the country of origin.

Every attempt has been made to contact the relevant copyright-holders,
but some were unobtainable. We would be grateful if the appropriate
people could contact us.

ACKNOWLEDGEMENTS

This book is dedicated to all of the following:

My mother, Dorothy.

My father, Karl. RIP.

My brother, Eric. RIP.

My stepmother, Colleen.

My children – Leonie, Bailey, Kye and Tyler, and my stepson Nathan. I love you all to the max.

My grandmother, Ina. RIP.

Auntie Flo and Auntie Pam. RIP.

My trainer, Dev Barrett – simply the best. Without you it couldn't have happened.

Andre – for always being by my side.

Todd and Rupert – brothers for life.

My good friend Malkit Singh.

My pals Longers and Jell (of the Zulus). RIP.

Harold and Cream Albert of the Rat Pack, and Wrigley of the Convicts. RIP.

Anthony Reid – aka Pastor Reid, long-time friend. Bless up!

The original Tiger Posse and the Townies – you know who you are.

My darling wife, Tracey Patterson – for believing in me and fighting my case.

My good friend Jason Kelsey – who is facing the biggest fight of his life. Bless.

All of my other friends and family – thank you for being there.

All of the people who have made me who I am today – all of my opponents, all of the football firms I battled with, and all of my enemies. LOL.

My legal team, Stefan and Lisa. Thank you for your work – if it wasn't for you, this book would be on hold.

All of my friends in Holland and around the world.

All of the Coventry and Birmingham massives.

And to BCFC – keep right on for life. *Zuluuuuuuuuu!!!!!!!!*

Barrington Patterson

INTRODUCTION

I've been training Barrington Patterson in Coventry for more than 20 years.

My name is Dev Barrett and I'm a karate and kickboxing instructor. I was born in Jamaica and came over to the West Midlands just after independence in 1963, when I was aged 10. I learned to fight at school because of the obvious problem that most people have as immigrants. I started playing rugby, which led me on to boxing, which everybody did in my day. That then led me to karate. I absolutely loved playing rugby at school and I also excelled at karate, so it was a tough decision to make the switch.

I started off in traditional karate and then I went on to kickboxing. In full-contact karate I went on to win the British title and European Challenge Cup title; I also became the first British fighter to win the world title in

ix

the ring. But I found kickboxing to be that little bit more 'honest'.

Karate was also good for discipline though. I worked as an electrician and became a foreman. I had a well-paid job and it was a tough decision, but I decided to give up work to focus on my sport fulltime. The sport was only at the amateur level, but what changed it was when my father passed away.

He worked all his life and didn't get to see much of us really. He finally took early retirement and went to Jamaica to look at some land; he wanted to go back. He was out there for three weeks and then he died. It seemed as if he didn't do much with his life and I decided I was going to do something I really liked.

In 1982, I gave up my job as an electrician to work as a fulltime teacher and trainer. In 1984, I opened up a gym in the city centre. At the time the local authorities were trying to get kids in the community into sport. There was always gang warfare going on in Coventry then.

A few years later, I was teaching a regular class. It was around 6.30pm and I remember it was as if the lights had gone out – when I looked round there were these two big fellows standing in the doorway. My immediate thought was: *Oh God!* because I'd heard that the week before somebody had come up and there was a bit of a problem with the other instructor that was teaching. So I obviously thought these two guys had come back to sort out whatever they had going on with him.

I ignored them for quite a while – I just continued teaching and they stood almost motionless in the doorway. I was teaching a class of young lads at the time and I remember thinking, *I hope it doesn't go off while they're here*. At the time I was a world champion and I didn't want to approach them in an aggressive way.

I was walking up and down the dojo, not saying anything to them as I was hoping they would go away, but then I thought, *Why? I'm a world champion*. I suddenly turned and looked at them and said, 'Can I help you?' There was a little bit of movement as if they were quite surprised at the way I approached them. The one in front filled the doorway, a huge black guy who must have been a bodybuilder; this was Barrington. The one behind was quite a bit bigger and taller, quite a smart-looking character. They called him 'Catalogue John', I found out later, because he looked like somebody who'd just walked out of a photo shoot.

They said they were interested in training, so I gave them the times, costs, etc. But I wasn't convinced; I thought, *There's a bit more to it*. I looked at them and I was thinking, *What do they want with martial arts, the size of them?*

I remember Barrington saying he just wanted to do some karate. Obviously I thought, *Thank God*. It was quite scary actually. At that point I thought, *We'll see*, but they did stay and watch for a while. After they left, I thought, *Maybe, maybe not*.

But they turned up the next time and that's how it all started; they both came and trained with me. Barrington is still with me today. He just trained as a regular student but, as time went on, he became an icon within the club because he seemed to gel with most other students. There was one group who seemed to get on with him really well, but there were others who seemed to be a bit wary of him because of his ways.

I always knew there was something about Barrington. Because you always have some characters in the world, a personality with a little bit of something different, like Muhammad Ali.

Barrington was one of those.

DEV BARRETT, former British, European and World W.A.K.O. (World Association of Kickboxing Organizations) full-contact champion

CHAPTER ONE

I never had any real problems at my first junior school, Farm Street in Hockley – which was later demolished. At home though, me and my sisters and brother all used to play around, argue and fight with each other all the time. It was competitive – with broomsticks, mops, whatever – but it never got to the stage where we pulled out knives on each other. None of us ever picked on an outsider either; it was always only each other.

One day, when I was seven, my sister Jennifer and I were playing in the garden. We often played together, as she was older than me by one year and she never had any fear of me. Jennifer is the oldest one over here – I've also got an older sister and brother in New York. She thought she ruled the roost – but I thought I did; I'm not the older one, I'm the bigger one!

ONE-EYED BAZ

On this particular day, we had an argument and, in anger, she dashed a full can of Coke at my head which caught me in my left eye. She meant to throw it *at* me – it was a woman's anger – but I'm she sure didn't mean it to cause the harm it did. I just felt the whack! And then I had blurred vision in my eye. It was like being punched on the jaw – you just feel a sharp pain. Then my mum took me aside, sat me down and put some water on my eye.

She could see something was wrong, and I was immediately rushed to A&E at Dudley Road hospital in Birmingham. At the time, the hospital had the nickname 'Slaughter House', because everyone who went there seemed to die, the thought of which was going through my seven-year-old mind. I was diagnosed as permanently blind in one eye that same night.

I never noticed anything different about my eyes though. I was young and I soon adapted, but to other people I became the playground joke. They called me 'One Eye', as my left eye was much smaller and obviously sightless. When I had my first fight, at eight years old, I got beaten up by two black kids of the same age who called me 'Cyclops'. I took a real beating; I felt really angry and went home to tell my mother, who cussed me in patois and told me, 'Fe gwan back out and fight back de bwoy!'

I never did. I was too scared and there were two of them, but it taught me a lesson and convinced me to get tougher. I continued to have playground scuffles at least once a week and would win nine times out of 10. I started to like it; I loved the buzz, and I firmly believe that this shaped my character into what it is today.

* * *

I was born on 25 August 1965. My mum, Dorothy Pearson, met and married my dad, Karl Kenneth Patterson, in Kingston, Jamaica. He first came over here in 1958, and then he brought my mum over to England to live with his mother, who was a nurse in Burton-on-Trent. My mum and dad had five kids together after my dad settled here, working in a factory. She already had two kids back in Jamaica – a boy named Christopher and a girl, Joy, who now lives in New York. When my mum came over here, she let Joy remain with her own mum's family, as was the way with so many Jamaicans who, like my mum and my father's mum, came to this country in search of a better life. Joy and Christopher made their own way. I keep in contact with Joy and visit her when I can, as I do with my stepbrother, who still lives in Jamaica.

After my parents settled in Burton-on-Trent, they went on to have five children. My sisters Jennifer and Sara and a sister who died of cot death in the 1970s, me and my brother Eric all had the Patterson surname. My mother would return to visit Jamaica on various occasions, but we lived in Burton until I was about four years old. We

3

lived in a house on a hill with a garden that backed on to fields, where there were horses and cows.

We had to move to Handsworth, Birmingham, where my mum's mother lived at the time. My dad had got into some trouble and was sentenced to eight years in prison. I never really knew my father until I was about 14 years old; before that I have little recollection of him at all. I knew from my mum that he was in prison and that was all I needed to know; as we were children, it was never discussed further. He'd had an argument with an Asian man who came to our house, and my dad grabbed a knife from the kitchen and stabbed him, something he confirmed to me later.

I have one other memory of Burton when I was a kid: it was before a visit to my grandmother's. My dad was still out of prison then and he was there when my mum tried to leave with us. He refused to let us go, but the police were called and we were escorted out.

Because my mum effectively became both Mum and Dad, and Gran was always around the house, I never felt that having my dad in prison affected me while I was growing up. I got the impression my dad was a bit of a rogue himself, from the stories he told me later when he came out of prison. For a time he'd lived in Bermondsey, south London, and it was a hard area with not many black people, where there would be scraps with teddy boys.

Handsworth was really multicultural in contrast to

where we'd just come from. When we moved into my grandmother's four-bedroom house in Lozells Road, I started to realise that there were more black people outside of my own immediate family – not just black, but Asian and other races too. The other change in my life was that my gran, Ina Johnson, took the role of my mum, now that she had to do several jobs to keep and sustain us all. The four of us had been brought up just by my mum and we never ever had a thing.

Then, a couple of years later, my aunt split up with her fella down in London, so she came to live with us as well. My sister Jennifer is a year older than me, Sarah is a year younger and my brother, Eric, was three years younger. With just a few years between us all, now we had our cousins living with us too – when my mum's sister got her divorce and moved in with five kids, who were all similar ages to us. Now there were three families in one house in Lozells, all trying to survive and look after one another. We used to take turns in sharing the beds and using the bathroom.

The Asian family living next door were the same – overcrowded. Everyone was, but you all got on. The Asian family used to bring some food over to the house; it was a close-knit community, black, Asian and white people were just as poor as each other. In Lozells, everyone was in it together and the only segregation was from the police. I'm a Lozells man – that was my area.

I had a good relationship with my mum but I had a lot

of energy as a boy. We were a typical Jamaican family that ran a strict household. If my gran said we had to go to church, then we had to go to church. It would be the sort of church where you'd vocally praise the Lord, with all this singing and shouting 'Hallelujah!' There would be church in the evening too, plus Sunday school, and you had to go: my grandmother used to say, 'No church, no dinner.' She had a big influence on us.

I stopped going to church when I was about 13; I felt old enough to make my own mind up. The rest of my family still attend and still try to convert me. I always say the same thing: 'The only time you will see me in church is funerals and weddings.' I believe in God – I just don't feel the need to go to church.

It wasn't easy growing up in a Christian family, what with being a football hooligan and getting nicked for fighting. You can imagine what my mum used to say! But she accepted it was my way of life and she always stood up for me – no matter what. She just accepted that's how my life was.

Amidst all the madness, my mum met and settled down with a nice bloke called Shaggy. He was a good man and they went on to have a daughter, Lorraine, who now lives with my mum and takes care of her since Shaggy passed away. I have a special bond with my half-sister and I've always had time for her.

* * *

Lozells is also the area where I went to school, at Farm Street. Those were the days of the Rastas and their sound systems: Observer, Eternal Youth, Jungleman, these were the sounds of the day. There was music coming from every street corner, like it was a festival every day. Rastas burning spliff stood on corners as police drove by; some guys didn't think about doing it undercover, it was like they wanted everyone to know.

I've always been into sports, rather than being academically minded. My first introduction to a fighting sport was after another scuffle, when I was nine or 10, and I walked past a local church-hall sign saying, 'Judo lessons here.' So the following week, I went along and joined there and then, just on my own. They made you wait and then you had to bow to everyone, including your opponent, and bow before you went into the dojo, which you couldn't enter with anything on your feet. It added a bit of discipline, because before that I was a bit of a rogue. This was something different to coming home and changing out of my school clothes to run around the street. I ended up doing judo two or three times a week there for five to six years, and I earned my purple belt before I stopped and went back to the streets.

My motivation for judo was that I wanted to learn how to fight properly and increase my ratio of wins to 10 out of 10. By this age I never wanted to lose a fight again.

MALKIT SINGH

My name's Mal, I'm from Salisbury Road in Handsworth. Barrington and me used to go to school together in the mornings, and in the evenings we used to do everything together, including training. We started judo together, with Mr Fields as the teacher. When Barrington used to go out he was concerned about people taking the Mickey out of him because of his eye, or getting bullied. By the time we were about 13 or 14 years old, he'd taken a lot of shit. He wasn't that big, no bigger than other kids, but there was this one guy, the school bully, who was six foot three. We'd get off the coach and we used to have to line up by the railings and wait for the teacher. Barrington was standing behind me and I was facing forwards when I heard this commotion and someone shouting, 'One Eye, One Eye!' Barrington got hold of the bully and was kicking the shit out of him before the teachers came along and stopped it.

That was a shock for me because I'd never seen him do that before. We'd just started judo but it wasn't like a contact sport, it was more throws and holds, but this was punching and kicking. He just really wanted to do the bloke; it was a good job the teacher came along. He must have flipped, but from that day on no one ever said anything insulting to Barrington again.

If there was a fight in school and Barrington was involved, then the whole school would watch. We'd seen him batter the cock of the school, a good fighter with big fists who not many people would want to take on; to see someone like that get the shit kicked out of him was a turning point. I seriously think that if that teacher hadn't stopped it Barrington would have killed him; he was on the floor and he was punching the daylights out of this big bully. He had loads of fights after that and everyone would be watching in a massive circle.

He was doing judo at school but he also started going to martial arts at a club outside. I wasn't going to those clubs, I was just doing it in school, but he really liked it.

Since we had moved from Burton, we had become very impoverished. I remember feeling different to other children. I had worn clothes passed down from neighbours and holes in my shoes; our Christmases and birthdays were all terrible. I never had any breakfast and part of my day consisted of thieving for food; I stole milk, cheese and bread from doors streets away from my house – but never in the same road, as that was disrespectful.

I broke into the Asian shops when I was eight or nine years old, stealing anything I could. I broke into warehouses with a couple of mates. Later, when I was about 12 or 13, we used to rob the punters who went to a rundown old pub round our way where the local prostitutes used to hang around. Whenever you saw the prostitute, you saw her punter, and we used to go and 'tax' that same punter to get easy money.

There was an area of Lozells where we knew the

prostitutes would hang out and we'd take money off them. Then we started to get friendly with them and said, 'Look, we can both make some money if we rob your punter.' I remember this brass sent us into a house with a client who was loaded. We already had two lads inside when she brought him; we came up behind, this Asian lad bashed him and we took all his money. I also mugged the prostitutes. I did whatever I could to survive.

Despite all this, I remember having good times at Hockley adventure playground, where I played happily as a kid. 'Horsemouth', a black guy, was a friend of mine that I'd been through all the same schools with, so we were pretty tight. But there was this other Asian lad whose parents had a corner shop, so he obviously had a bit of poke (cash) on him. Horsemouth and me thought it was a good idea to hold him up – I can't remember who had the knife, but we stopped him and took all his biscuit money. Word got around, the headmaster found out and we got suspended from school. Our mothers had to come down: Horsemouth's mum started going on about how I was a bad influence upon her son and I remember her bashing him silly.

When I left junior school, I had a good friend named Robert Luca, a white punk rocker. We did a lot of things together and he joined me on my first day at senior school. But in week one Robert got expelled for smacking a teacher in the face. From that day till this, I have never seen him again. I made some lifelong friends in school though – including Anthony Reed, who's now a pastor and who taught me how to ride a bike at 11. (Late starter, I know.)

I continued to fight my way through senior school; some memorable times include sports days and athletics days, when we visited other schools. I would take on the hardest boy I could see and try to make a name for myself. It often turned into a big tear-up with loads of people fighting – great fun.

I was arrested for the first time at 11 years old. There was me and three other guys, and we decided to break into this builder's yard just to see what we could get. We climbed through the fence and smashed our way into their office with a brick, starting to fumble through the drawers and throwing things all over the place. All of a sudden, after about 15 minutes, a torch shone through. It was the police, shouting, 'Come out! Come out!'

I started shitting myself because we'd never done this before. We were debating what we were going to do as the police came into the builder's yard and grabbed us. I was really scared because we'd never had a confrontation like this, but I was more scared of the beating from my mum.

They took us all down to Thornhill Road police station. They interviewed us and then my mum came down, very upset. It was serious – we were getting charged with burglary. We later made a couple of appearances before the courts, where I pleaded guilty, but

I got a beating off my mum. I got an even worse one when I got found guilty and let off with a fine. I thought, *I ain't going to let this happen again!*

MAL
We didn't have much money in those days. I'd bought this bike and I needed five quid and I couldn't have asked my dad, he'd just have given me a beating and said, 'Don't buy things you can't afford!' I told Barrington and he said, 'We'll get it, we'll get it!' He wanted us to rob a chemist's shop. Barrington was ready to do it, but I bottled it. He said, 'I do it all the time, that's why I get arrested!' I didn't do that sort of stuff, but it was like second nature to him.

When I was 12, my mother took us out to a local picture-house called the Grand Palace on Soho Road. This was the first time I had seen a kung fu film and I was immediately mesmerised; I came out of the pictures thinking, *I want to be like Bruce Lee*. There were two cinemas in our area, the Grand Palace and Elites. Every Friday and Saturday night, they would be screening kung fu films, so me and my cousin would get our chips and sit through the show from 12 o'clock until 4 or 5am in the morning. You'd come out of the picture-house and everyone was making all these noises and doing kung fu moves in the street.

That started my love affair with martial arts. From that moment I always wanted to do something like that, so I started shotokan karate lessons at a school for a couple of years, but I didn't like the style. My friends and I continued to go to the pictures every week though, and after the screening we used to mimic Bruce Lee and his fighting techniques. I remember those as very happy times.

* * *

I never saw my dad again until I was 14. I remember one day my mum had a letter that she was reading in the kitchen, but, when I walked in, she threw it in the bin.

I got it out of the bin. It was a letter from the courts in London, regarding access and maintenance. It had a court date on it, so me and my mate jumped the train to London with not a penny in our pockets. We bunked the train and stayed in the toilets (as you did in those days).

All I had was an old picture of my dad that my grandmother had given me, but we made it to the courthouse and I found my dad's name on the door of the courtroom. When we walked in, I saw a black guy and a woman sitting outside and I knew instantly it was my dad. He later said that, as soon as he saw me, he knew it was his son, Barrington.

After the court case, we went back to my dad's flat. His wife, Colleen, gave us a good feed and put us on the train back home.

From that day, I started to build a relationship with my dad. We kept in contact, and I always used to visit during the school holidays. Colleen treated us well and I looked forward to those visits as a kid.

I was going out to get money myself and I'd ring my dad sometimes to say I was coming to London. At the time, my dad was working as a presser in a laundry, while Colleen used to work emptying fruit machines; so I used to go down sometimes at a weekend and do some work with Colleen, then come back and spend some time with my dad. He'd take me round the area of London where they were living, telling me stories about how he used to be a rude boy in the area. I'd keep going up there but my brother and sisters weren't really interested in my dad at all; I was the only one who kept going backwards and forwards. I was just doing my own thing anyway. But even before my dad died they weren't really bothered, they wouldn't go down and see him.

Still, to this day, I have a close relationship with my step-mum. She will always be a big part of my life and she says it's strange how I'm so much like my dad, considering I grew up without him.

He was a bodybuilder and he was into martial arts – it must be in the blood.

CHAPTER TWO

I started getting braver and venturing out of Handsworth into the big city of Birmingham with my good pal Thomas Coley. We were part of a gang called the Handsworth Wanderers who used to go to the Bull Ring in Birmingham and hang around the ramp and fountain, at the entrance to New Street train station where all travellers into Birmingham had to come. (This is where I would base myself in my Zulu days, later in my life.)

At the Bull Ring, we were fighting, robbing and taxing whoever we could. Our numbers swelled and there were now over 50 of us. My reputation was growing too; I wasn't aware of it, as I was a follower not a leader, but people were scared of me and did what I said. I used to have dreadlocks, little picky locks, as was the style if you came from Handsworth. Our gang had some terrifying people – whether we were Rasta, Asian or white guys, we feared no one. We just loved to fight and make money. We would attack every football fan that came into the centre, no matter where they were from. People used to hate coming into Birmingham because they knew the risk of getting taxed, or of a knife being pulled and them getting slashed by us.

I can't play football to save my life. It had never really interested me and it might have stayed that way. But football came to me when I was a rude boy, hanging uptown on a Saturday night during the early eighties. My pal Horsemouth ran with the rude boys; we would wear the two-tone gear and pork-pie hats, short trousers and brogues, so we were a kind of mixture of mods and skins – but we didn't really get on with the mods or the skinheads, with their long Parka coats or big Doc Marten boots with coloured braces. We were into ska music, the Coventry band The Specials, The Selecter and all that. We'd go to gigs in town to see bands like The Beat; we'd steam the clothes shops for our gear and be wearing it the same night. One lad would walk in the shop and steal a rack of clothes; nobody would chase him because he'd have five lads behind him to stop anyone when he walked out. We were the rude boys, we did what we had to do to make a bit of poke for ourselves and to enjoy ourselves.

There used to be about five of us from Handsworth and we'd meet up with other lads to go out on the town on a Friday and Saturday night, or fight with the skinheads and mods on a Saturday afternoon. Town was our base and that was where we used to hang out and earn our money.

We were now part of a larger gang with more clout, called the Townies, and we used this as cover for 'draipsing' (taking designer clothes and jewellery off the rich kids). This led to us running the town; it was our manor and no one could trouble us. We were about 20-to-30-strong, with people like Rupert, a really good friend who's been like a second brother to me, plus Todd, Rupert's cousin who lives in Tamworth, Louis, Skan, Sharkey and Curly. As Birmingham was our domain, we used to rob football supporters – sometimes even the Apex, who were Birmingham City supporters. We had no morals.

I used to notice all these skinheads coming into town and wonder where the heck they were all coming from. We soon learned they were Apex and as rude boys we just said, 'Fuck 'em, skinheads are racists,' but we'd see this black skinhead with them from time to time and say: 'Hey, what's that nigger doing with them skinheads?' We'd chase him as well and, to be honest, he would get a worse kicking for being black. So, after every match on a Saturday, when all the skinheads used to come through town, we'd have it off with them – even some of the Apex. We used to have it with their lot all the time – that's how we got into the football. Then we started attacking all the away fans that were coming to town.

At that time we weren't really interested in football. We were Townies and only interested in making some fucking poke and having fun! The Bull Ring shopping centre was the place where we hung out, fought and earned our money before and during the match, which was why more police were brought into the Bull Ring, as on most Saturdays while everyone was out shopping, you would have people running and screaming.

RUPERT & TODD

Rupert: *We liked The Specials*

Todd: *It was the Two Tone ska, the old blue beat music, and it was kind of like a switchover where white and black music met together.*

Rupert: *From the Midlands you had The Beat, The Selecter.*

Todd: *I think at the time we were quite heavily into that. But Barrington, because he was from the ghetto, it was only natural to put a beret on his head and a pair of short trousers on and be a Rasta. Barrington was the only Rasta I knew who ate pork – LOL! – and I think that's what made us kind of know that he was from round there but he was more like us! It didn't take him long to become like us, I can remember when Barrington joined the firm.*

Rupert: *It didn't take him a long time at all.*

Todd: *I think this punk lad who disappeared, called 'Luke' (Robert Luca), was Barrington's friend. I saw Luke's mate Lamb the other week and he told me that*

Luke had died from a drug overdose. When we were rude boys in town it was because of Luke and Lamb that we could interact with the punks and the skinheads.

Todd: *I know that Luke was very influential with the punks; he was one of the main punk lads. I used to go down there all the time, because at the time you had all the rude girls and the half-skinhead girls, but when you wanted to interact with the punk girls, who you never saw much of because they were with the skinheads, you could go and talk with Luke who was mates with them all. There was one black guy who was a skinhead; when the skinheads and the punks and rude boys started to mingle then the blacks came in.*

Rupert: *If the Birmingham skinheads would fight with anybody they'd fight with us, and we'd fight the mods.*

Todd: *It was massive! Down by the library we used to have running battles; there were probably about 300 on each side and the rockers were getting it too. I can remember times when we all used to go down there: me, Rupert, Barrington and a few more of them; there was a guy called Terry, who used to think he was 'the face' of the mods, and he used to come up and try to mix with us and find out what we were doing but, depending on what mood we were in, he'd probably end up getting a slap! Nine times out of 10 it would be Barrington who gave him a slap.*

Rupert: *He was older than us, he was twice our age.*

Todd: *It was a really crazy time! I can remember once I*

*took his Parka and we all went down to Bingley Hall. All
the rude boys stayed hidden and I walked up towards the
mods, dressed in his Parka, saying, 'The rude boys are
coming!' As soon as the mods got near, the rude boys
jumped out and we had a running battle with the mods.*
Rupert: *That was just up the road from the police station.
They used to have all the Vespas and Lambrettas parked
there and we used to kick their bikes over!*

On a Saturday you used to get loads of lads coming into
the town, so we thought it was a good way to earn a bit
of poke. We used to tax them; we'd take them to one side
and take their money off them – if they had nice clothes
on, we'd take them too. Then we'd give them a little slap
and send them on their way.

The main place we'd hang out would be either by the
fountain or the ramp, which was where everyone headed
from the train station. We'd have a group of around 20
rude boys and rude girls and there were other gangs
scattered around who hung out near the fountain, e.g. the
Jazz Funkers (aka the Convicts), the Rat Pack, who hung
out in the Night Rider pub, and also the Apex. Sometimes
fights could break out between us, but, if outsiders came
into town, the Townies and the other gangs formed
alliances. This is how the Zulus started to form, from
different gangs joining forces against rival football firms
coming into our city.

I was living in Handsworth at the time but I was in

town every day. I'd finish at school, get home, change and head straight into town, then I'd catch the last bus home at about 11.30–12. We had to earn money, so it was in town that I had my little earners.

On Saturday, in came all the football fans who we'd started taxing. Then, all of a sudden, you started getting these skinheads coming into town. We'd wait for 'em to walk through and we'd hammer 'em – bang 'em, bang 'em, *bang* 'em! But there was this black guy who used to hang around with them. He was a local skinhead and I used to think, *Fucking coconut, man!*

RUPERT & TODD

Todd: *Barrington's always been like a human version of a 'staff', a Staffordshire bull terrier. You'll get a lot of dogs that'll fight if they're under pressure, but the staff was bred to fight and with Barrington it's the same, he's just always liked fighting. From the age of 16, when I met him, we had a couple of lads in the firm that could have a good old fight but no one was like Barrington. He had no fear, not even of the police, he just didn't care! We were kids at the time, growing up, sometimes we'd have trouble with girls' parents and they'd come down. They were big, strapping blokes, but, as soon as they stepped up to Barrington, me and Rupert would look at each other, put our hands over our mouths and say, 'I don't think this geezer realises what he's let himself in for!' A lot of the time people would come down for Barrington with weapons and he would take the weapon off them and beat them. Don't get me wrong: he's a lovely guy and he's got a big heart and he's a very good friend to have. But he's a very, very bad enemy to have. Before Barrington was onside with us in our firm, he came from the ghetto with a predominantly Asian firm: a few Chinese, a few blacks, including a bloke called Thomas Coley. As soon as him and Thomas came into town all the boys knew that the Handsworth Wanderers were here. I think the only words I can remember Barrington saying at the time were, 'Do you want a fight?' LOL! Nothing else! He'd look at you with his eye and say, 'D'you wanna fight?'*

Rupert: *In the early eighties, there was a big black community in Handsworth, but there was a big Indian community as well.*

Todd: *You could say that at the time Handsworth was a bit of a criminal community like many areas in Birmingham, but a lot of people would turn around and say, 'What are you putting Handsworth down for?' I suppose it comes down to the circles that you move in, not the area you're from. In Handsworth, there were more blacks than other areas; where I came from it was pretty much 50 per cent black/50 per cent white. Where Barrington came from it was 80 per cent black/20 per cent white, so when you've got black around black it makes you more 'urban'.*

Rupert: *I lived in a white area, in Quinton. At that time*

we were still at school; the first day I went into that playground and said my name, it was like BANG! I remember a day when we went to a Birmingham game; me and Barrington were there and this was before the Zulus and all that lot. That was the day I saw the change in our generation coming through, because all the guys older than us were white guys.

Todd: *And the funny thing about it is that when we came into town, as 15-year-olds, the first thing we did was stamp out the racism that was around in the early eighties and there was a lot of it about. A lot of people had to be put in their places as times were changing and we were helping them change. Barrington was in the ghetto at the time, knocking someone else's head off – thank God for that! As we got into the mods and rockers scene, that's when Barrington came along and we used to have some good battles; in those days, there would be a good few hundred of us. There were a few of us who were tight-knit, 10 to 15 of us who were just the firm on our own and that's when Barrington came into it. We had several names before we got named the Townies – like Rudies, Tiger Posse, Nigger Squad. But when I wasn't in town people used to say, 'Watch out for the Townies, if you're in town you'll get robbed' – not realising I was a Townie.*

I can remember a time when we were walking through Handsworth and Barrington looks across the road and sees this guy. He says, 'That guy over there used to bully me when I was at school,' and he hadn't seen him since then. But obviously since then his confidence had built up. He walks over to the guy, who was several years older than him, and says, 'Oi, pussy! D'you remember me? D'you remember you used to bully me at school?'

And the guy's looked at Barrington and I think he could smell the fierceness of him. He just scurried on as fast as he could!

When I was a kid at school I did get bullied over my eye, but years later I'd bump into certain people and give them a slap for it. That's how long I hold a grudge – for years.

RUPERT & TODD

Todd: *When we were 17, we used to mess about in the Pallasades shopping centre, sometimes we used to do the security's heads in. There was one security guard called 'Shotgun Tommy' and we used to take the piss out of him all the time, even though he was a really nice guy; we used to call him Urko because he was built like the gorilla from Planet of the Apes, I'm telling you. Solid! One day he just says to Barrington, 'If you think you're tough let's go round the back for a straightener!' and I'm telling you, that was a fight and a half. He looked at us after and looked at Barrington and said, 'Him tough!' I know Barrington thought,* Well, this man's tough himself, *but Barrington was only 17.*

Rupert: *I remember when they used to have the cameras there and there was this one security guy we used to call*

'Shitty Batty'. He must have told us to move on or something; it was late at night because the shops were closed. Someone must have started arguing the case, saying, 'There's no one around, so what are you moving us on for?' So they've got into a bit of a set-to and Barrington and him have decided to sort it out. Barrington's moved the camera so that it's facing the other way. Then he fucking mullahed him!

Todd: 'The Bear' was this lad who used to knock around within the firm but he was a lot older than us – he was the biggest by far. A few lads in the firm kind of feared him because he was a bit of a bully at times to some of the weaker crew members, but he came in very handy at times when we had problems with rival firms. Some of them stayed away from him and some of them let him buy drinks for them to try to buy their friendship that way, but he always ended up turning. Probably the last day he ever turned on anyone was when we were walking back to the station and he started picking on Rupert a bit. Everyone was getting a bit concerned; you had to be careful because if you picked on certain members of the firm then the other lads were going to feel like, 'You're picking on me as well.' Some members of the firm carried a bit more clout and they weren't meant to be bullied. Rupert was one of them.

I think that day Barrington had no other option but to fight him. They had a fight and a half. There was this place called Wade's, they used to sell carpets and they *had a balcony there. Barrington chucked him over the balcony then went down and carried on. The Bear bit out a chunk of Barrington's arm and they had a serious fight that day, but in Barrington's head it's never ever been over. He always says to me, 'See what I'll do – if I ever see him again I'll batter the head off him!' Me and Barrington were working together later in security; I actually brought him back to Birmingham to work. There was a problem in my mate's shop with some of the young gang members; the gaffer was having trouble with them so we came back to Birmingham to try to solve the situation. That's when The Bear stopped coming to town – when he found out Barrington was back in Birmingham.*

Rupert: *It was because he had that fight with Thomas first, do you remember?*

Todd: *Thomas Coley was Barrington's partner from when he first came to Birmingham. I think at the time Thomas was actually tougher than Barrington, he was a nasty piece of work – but he became a very good friend of mine and still is! When you saw him coming and you saw Barrington behind him, you thought,* Shit!

Rupert: *They were in the same class at school and they both got expelled.*

Then we got to know some of these skinhead guys and we started talking. Before you knew it, the fashion changed so quickly that by the next football season you would

26

notice all these dressers come into town wearing Tacchini, Fila, Ellesse and all that. Then the London club guys would come in with their Pringle and Armani and Lacoste and we'd think, *We can't afford all those fucking things!* But they were on our manor so we taxed 'em.

At most of the matches we'd go to, we'd have a little earner. Sometimes we would send the lads to have a fight so that they could distract the police; we would leave them and go to the pub, wreck it and break open any fruit or fag machines. The same if it was a shop – we would go in to steam it, grabbing whatever we wanted.

It was around this time that there was a major problem within the black community. We were treated like shit, the police had no respect for us, and all the black and Asian families were dumped into the ghettoes of Birmingham. I guess it had happened in other places as well, like Toxteth and Brixton, but we were acutely aware of the underlying issues as we experienced them day after day and we were involved in the Handsworth riots. We had the idea that, if we created enough chaos, we could make some money – as all the shopkeepers would abandon their shops. That was our way of life. We came about 20-handed and all we were interested in was breaking into shops and taking what we could.

Sometimes you just wanted to destroy things; other times you'd run into a shop and come out with things you didn't even need, running straight home, putting it away in the house and running back out again. You would have maybe one room full up with stolen goods, including quite a few things you'd never had before. Then your house would get raided.

That first night of the riots, we all arranged to meet up at the top of Handsworth and plan what we were going to do. The police had the SPG (Special Patrol Group) at the time and they were just bastards. All they wanted was to beat people with their long truncheons, and you knew that when the SPG were coming you had to run.

Everything was directed against the police. We just wanted to tell people what they were like and what they were doing, but nobody wanted to take it onboard. It was like a cry for help – people knocked Handsworth, Toxteth and Brixton, but all they remember about those areas is the riots. If they hadn't actually lived there, then they didn't know what they were like. Handsworth had as nice a community as anybody else's area.

It was a nice feeling too – people were trying to put their point across because the government were not interested. Everyone was trying to get the aggression out of themselves, because in those days a black lad could be walking down the street and he would get stopped for no apparent reason. Or he would be told to get out of his car; the black guy would turn round and say, 'Why? I ain't done nothing,' and the police would hold up a bag of weed and say they found it in the car. They were well known for planting drugs on people and saying it was theirs.

Most of the towns that rioted back in 1981 did so for a reason – not like the recent riots around the UK in August 2011, after the police shot and killed Mark Duggan. People just wanted to be heard as they were putting up with a lot of shit in those days. But for us it was just about money, money, money. We weren't into that aspect – we were into the looting.

Riots are riots at the end of the day, but they're not like they used to be years ago. Some of the guys go over the top with the rioting – setting fire to people's houses and things like that. When we were rioting we were just grabbing things, we weren't setting light to the premises; we were just providing things for our families – or for ourselves, or whatever. Fuck burning down a big store when there are people living on top of the fucking building!

While the riots were on, we made a lot of money. We looted shops of their stock, including food, fags, booze, furniture, TVs, anything that we could. But one of the sad things that came out of the riots was that my good friend, Thomas Coley, got jumped on by the SPG and beaten very badly. Thomas had a promising career ahead of him as a boxer and was due to represent England; his beating changed that and he's never been right again. He was one of the guys I used to look up to, coming from Handsworth. He was a wicked fighter, but when the SPG got him in the riots they fucking hammered him.

RUPERT & TODD

Todd: *Barrington came from Handsworth and when he came up into the city he had the Handsworth mentality; they used to go up to the skinheads and take their boots off them, and their laces! But Barrington kind of turned. He left the Handsworth lot and started to hang around with us lot in town. He started going to the football, shoplifting, everything that we were doing as kids, which progressed into the football violence and meeting women, and his life kept on accelerating to where he is now.*

Rupert: *Barrington always had money, he always worked. I wish I was like that. Anyone he met or had a bond with, he would keep in contact with.*

Todd: *He had a job, he always had money, and he always had a missus. His only downfall at the time was gambling, he'd always be across the road in The Night Rider and he'd be playing cards: blackjack and brag. Barrington was our mate but we couldn't get in the way of his gambling, because if we went to the pub where he was gambling with the older lot he'd tell us to piss off! But he was the only one who had a job and he was in a stable relationship; he thought so much of the girl he was with at the time, I'm surprised he never ended up marrying her. She was a blonde-haired girl from Erdington, wasn't she?*

As kids, we never really knew about designer clothes and, even if we did, we couldn't afford those things. I remember your Adidas four-stripe and wearing an Adam and the Ants T-shirt. We'd go to school in plimsolls with the cardboard pushed down inside to try to stop the water soaking through, and side-pocket trousers with a big utility belt.

When the shops finally took notice of all this designer stuff and started to stock all these smart tracksuits, a big sports shop opened up. On the first day it opened, we broke into it and robbed all the tracksuits – Ecko, Ellesse, Sergio Tacchini. Before that I was wearing Adidas, with the four-stripe trainers, and in town people would be taking the piss out of me. People all around, including us, started to come out of wearing Sta-Press and brogues and became a bit more casually dressed.

It had mainly been a music scene, but then all the casual clothes started coming in. You had all these shops opening in Birmingham like Cecil Gee and other shops were selling Gabicci and all that. As soon as the shops opened, we were breaking into them and robbing them. On a Friday or Saturday, you'd just walk in and take a handful of clothes. You'd walk out and nobody could stop you. We continued steaming into designer shops and taking all the stock out – Armani jeans, Nevica skiwear, Tacchini and Fila tracksuits. In and out in one minute, that was our aim. Then there were all the guys coming from London wearing Tacchini and Fila. We just taxed them and took it off them.

Now that we'd started to go places, some of the ex-skinheads we knew would ask, 'Why don't you come to a game?' So we started to go down to the football match; that was where it all began.

RUPERT & TODD

Rupert: *I remember when we were playing Arsenal; we'd just come off the bus and we were walking up towards the ground. We had a little set-to with some Arsenal fans but the funny thing about the story was that they'd come running up behind us, Barrington's done a roundhouse, knocked the geezer out and one of the lads that was with us started rifling through his pockets!*

That was about '82. The big turning point was when we started getting the lads from Birmingham town, the Townies, going to Birmingham football games. Mickey Francis wrote about it in his book, Guvnors. *Man City, who were called the Cool Cats at the time, came walking past McDonald's in the centre. We'd already had word, because in those days there were no mobile phones so we always had spies out. Some of the lads have come along and said, 'City are here and they're walking through the shopping centre.'*

Todd: *In those days, it was individual firms on every corner; sometimes it would get a bit frisky and we'd interact with them and get shirty, ending up having a fight if one person had a problem with someone else from another firm. This was before the Zulus, when we were generally fighting with the Apex who were*

Birmingham's City's firm at the time, along with other local firms.

Rupert: *A lot of the time when we'd come uptown, we brought a lot of attention to ourselves. We were young and we all came from different parts of Birmingham, so at the time some of us were Villa, some of us were West Brom, but we weren't that interested in football.*

Todd: *At the time, I don't think we really cared about the football; we were more into violence and raising money. We got into the football violence because the fans would have to come through New Street station and the first people they got to before they found the Apex were us – the Townies.*

Rupert: *When Man City came walking through, it was the first time I'd ever seen a black firm come into Birmingham. We just swamped 'em. Those that didn't get away got slapped. They try to make out that they came back later and did us, but they didn't because we were there till 11 o'clock at night on the ramp. They got smashed. A few weeks later, we played Everton; they came through and there was this Rasta on the floor, the police had him and pulled his locks out! Now Everton appeared from out of nowhere and chased a few lads around the corner: guess who was there? They were running into it so fast that they got it big-time, they got the worst beatings. Barrington was always there, he was always involved. After Man City and Everton, the other teams that came through were Tottenham and Millwall.*

The last time I went to Man City was about five years ago, on the anniversary of the 1982 formation of the Zulus. A big firm of us went up there and took their main fucking pub.

We met up with a black guy called Fanny, originally from Birmingham but now living in Manchester, who supports Man City. There were no rows before the match but afterwards it kicked off quite a bit. We later heard from Fanny that Man City admitted no firm had ever gone there and taken them on like we did – not even Man United.

RUPERT & TODD

Todd: *Even when we were still in small groups we would be chanting, 'Zulus!' when we were running into people. At that time, the football was still predominantly white.*
Rupert: *We were the first generation that went down there to St Andrew's. I remember me and Barrington walking to the ground and suddenly realising we were surrounded by Villa. Barrington was at the front because at the time he was the most recognisable to the Villa fans; if he ever came into town he was always getting spotted by other firms. He had this almost mythical thing about him, so people were always wary of coming up to him because he would stand there toe-to-toe and have a row. So we're walking up and Barrington's gone, 'There's Lloydy,' who was one of their top boys, and I've thought,* Oh shit! *Barrington*

looked round to me as if to say, 'I'm going to swerve him – he's my cousin!'

We would fight football fans on Saturdays and I always noticed the black skinhead. We got talking and started going down to the matches together. This was around the same time as black ska fans and white punks all started mixing together due to our common interests of fighting, music and football. Before then I'd had no interest in football. There were no black people down at the matches, apart from us Townies and the black skinhead. So we linked up, which was how the Zulus were formed.

I remember the first match I went to. I thought, *Fucking hell, it's just full of white people!* You could count the black people on two bloody hands! But it was a good game and there was no trouble. We started going to watch football from then on and did so for years. The first game where I had a row was against Arsenal. I was outside the ground and I gave this guy a spinning hook kick. He just landed on his head and from that point all the fighting started.

The 82/83 season was when the Zulu thing started with Manchester City. We were all individuals. Even though I was from Handsworth, I came with the Townie lot; we had guys from Chelmsley Wood, which is a main place for skinheads. We had the little Acocks Green firm and the Sheldon firm. All different lads from different areas.

When people hear about the Zulus, they think it's a

black thing, but it's always been a multiracial thing – a Birmingham City thing, and that's how we'll keep it. We used to just meet up at a couple of pubs via word of mouth. We'd go down to where Villa drank, give it to them down there and go back to our pub. Everybody always said that the city was divided between Blues and Villa, but it's never been like that. It's always been a Blues place. They used to come down to our manor and they'd get hammered and sent back out of town.

There are certain places in Birmingham that Villa won't come, whereas Blues will go anywhere in town, like the Arcadia club. The same goes for the players: Blues players will go out anywhere in Birmingham but the Villa players won't; they'll probably go to places like Sutton Coldfield, but in Birmingham they'd get 'clattered'.

RUPERT & TODD

Rupert: *Remember Sutton Coldfield?*

Todd: *Yeah, we used to go down there when we started travelling out of town, getting a bit more adventurous!*

Rupert: *We used to go down there because they had a mob that ran with Villa and we needed Barrington down there. Because we were young, they could overpower us, but we'd keep going. If we had a fight and Barrington wasn't there, we wished he was because he was like the strength in the firm.*

Todd: *We even went through periods where we used to have competitions to see who could knock the most people out. Barrington would say he'd done the most and I'd say, 'No you haven't, I have,' and then Rupert would say he'd done the most but one of the others would say, 'Yeah, but that geezer wasn't completely unconscious!' We were young and reckless.*

Rupert: *At West Ham v Birmingham 1984, I remember we were at the game and Barrington got kicked out. I also remember one night these Man Utd lads came walking past and started getting cocky. So we had words and they've gone, 'See ya!' Barrington and this other guy went and fucking wasted 'em! They gave it to 'em big-time just round the ramp on the entrance to the shopping centre. This was in 82/83. Boy, did they get beat!*

I just love fighting! Anything for a fight! I was never interested in the game – I was just interested in a row before and after. I don't really like football; pussies play football and roll around on the floor.

CHAPTER THREE

I remember my first game, in the 82/83 season, and thinking, *There are no niggers here!* My first away games came a season later and then I was going to any big game after that; I can remember going to Leeds and being ambushed. I remember some games where I absolutely shat myself.

Leeds at home, Leeds away, West Ham at home, Millwall away twice – fucking hell, out of all the matches, that is the one that stands out more than any other!

All we heard about Millwall was that they were just like Leeds – a bunch of racists! We thought they were among the top dogs in London, but we always rated West Ham and Tottenham higher at the time. Everyone was geared up, but guys from the black and Asian communities were *really* geared up for Millwall.

I left work early that day and met up with the lads in town. 'We ain't buying a fucking train ticket! There's a couple of hundred of us going down there.' We went straight through the barriers and got on to the train. Some of the lads bought a McDonald's and others had cans of lager for the train, but there was a big police presence. We had a firm of 200-to-400-strong and everyone was up for the fucking row.

Everyone sat on the train chilling out, playing cards and cracking jokes. It took us about an hour and a half to get to Euston station. As soon as we got off the train, the police had their own fucking firm there! They were taking photos, asking our names and where we were from. Everyone had scarves over their faces, but they were telling us that anyone covering his face would be arrested.

I had a Burberry shirt and jacket, blue jeans and trainers and a scarf over my face. We were just about to break off from the police escort when they shouted, 'Come 'ere, lads! You're with this lot, ain't ya?'

We had a bit of a reputation at this time because we'd stood with a couple of top-rated English firms. So we thought that not only would we be facing Millwall but that we'd also have to fight other London teams – probably West Ham and Spurs. The police put us on another train to the Millwall ground, but we managed to break off and meet up with a couple of guys from Birmingham who now lived in London. Around 20 of us managed to get out of the pub and through a back door, then fucked off and left the rest with the police escort.

We stayed close by so we could see where the escort was and what was happening. Then the police put us on this train to Bermondsey. As we pulled up, all we could hear was *boom – boom*! The train was being fucking bricked! I'd never been to Millwall's ground but I could see it was near a fucking rough housing estate. Through every little corner you could see a firm. The police had their riot shields, but we were being bricked from every corner of the ground. They marched us into the ground, close to the pitch, then put us in an upper tier. We were behind the goal and some of us black lads took our shirts off. They were shouting, 'Fucking niggers!' We were shouting, 'Sieg heil!' A lot of Millwall were singing to Birmingham, 'You've got a town full of Pakis!' When Birmingham scored we were singing, 'One-nil to Pakistan!'

Nothing could really go off in the ground, so we just stood there laughing. We were singing our songs about what was going to happen when we got outside, how we were going to have it with 'em. We gave 'em the 'Sieg heil! Sieg heil!' and you could see they just fucking hated it. The atmosphere inside that ground was electrifying. The police tried to lock us all in about 15 minutes before the game's end, but I left with the final 15 minutes to go. The police said they were going to keep the Blues behind after the game, but we started fighting them and breaking down doors. We just wanted to get out and get at fucking Millwall!

All of a sudden, the gates opened and it was like a battleground, like derelict buildings on a bombsite. There were bricks everywhere, cars turned over and a police horse had been fucking slashed and was lying on the ground! A big firm of us had to walk down to the train station, through a housing estate, and guys were popping up everywhere to try to brick us. They were throwing bricks, bottles, bangers – it was like a proper fucking warzone! This was on a whole different level. Some of the lads were glad the police were there, otherwise someone would have died. They were protecting us with their riot shields. We got on to the train and even that got smashed up – it was bricked from the outside and *we* smashed it up on the inside.

Even today, people still talk about that day at Millwall. It was one of the worst ever. It was football violence but there was no actual clash between us. And Millwall didn't like it because they couldn't get to us, so they smashed their manor up. We were shocked because there were bricks coming from all different angles, but I think the police were scared. Millwall didn't come out and fight us though. It's not as if they stood in front of us saying, 'Let's 'ave it!' And if they had, we'd have been a big enough, game enough firm that day.

* * *

Another game that sticks with me was when we went to Tranmere, another cup game. I've never been called 'nigger sunshine' in my life, before or since. We had a cup match away at Tranmere and a firm-and-a-half turned up for it. We travelled up by train and car. I was still living in Handsworth at the time and some of the guys, including Big Chest Leroy and Rupert, came round to mine. About five of us went in my car. We met up with others in town but everyone shot off at different times. We drove our cars up to a service station outside Liverpool – where we had a laugh and were chatting up the girls – and called taxis to take us into Tranmere.

I think we got there around 11am. People could tell we were from out of town. From inside the car, we'd ask them where the football ground was, but they just didn't want to talk to us. People would walk off and ignore us, five black lads in a car, wondering, *What the fucking hell is going on?* We drove on and asked a group of lads where the ground was. 'There's no fuckin' darkies up 'ere!' was their answer.

One of the lads tried to jump out of the car, totally furious, but they warned us, 'No! You can't do that around 'ere!' Just walking down the streets, you'd see a bunch of lads and it was, 'Darkie! Darkie! Darkie over there!'

As soon as the police clocked us, they were round us like flies around shit. They locked us in a pub but some of us managed to get out. I got out before the start of the game and it was going off all over the place. We sent some guys over to have a row, so that the police went over to them while we were breaking into the fruit machines. In those days, it was expensive to go up there, so you had to make your money back. We took the machines off, bashed them and raided them.

We must have been in there a good hour-and-a-half before the police said we had to start making our way to the ground. Everyone started walking and just having a laugh in a firm of about 200 of us. All these Tranmere fans that we had to pass were giving it the wanker sign and more or less all you could hear was 'niggers', etc. Even during the match, all you got off the Tranmere guys was 'darkies' and 'coons'. There were a few skirmishes but everyone got into the ground, where the police started to get all agitated and lashed out at us with truncheons. It was clear to me that neither the fans nor the police had ever seen so many black lads at the football in their life and appeared to feel threatened by us.

RUPERT

Rupert: *I was in Tranmere with him one year on the last game of the season. I always remember that day: we had the end behind the goal and there were no police but for some stupid reason, halfway through the game, they wanted to come in but the boys wouldn't let them in so it went off between them. They'd been looking on the cameras and trying to target certain members of the firm. After the game, me and Barrington are in the park and all these police have pulled out of nowhere and gone hurtling down the road, so we've pulled out and followed them. They've all gone into this petrol station and everyone at that station got beats. The police gave it to them and they were all dressed like Robocop.*

We went to the game and there were a few rows, but nothing much. Then we came out and it just went off! All you could hear was: 'The darkies are over there!'

Later, we heard that Tranmere were up the road; we all rolled out of the pub and went to find them. They had a firm of around 50; some of them were real dressers but some were like tramps from a local estate.

We were in some boozer without any character at all, near the train station. Someone walked in and said, 'They're over there' – across the road from the pub. We all piled out and had our bottles ready, lined up on some road on a council estate. It was really rough, with boarded-up windows and houses with no curtains. It was a really trampy area.

I think there were about 70–80 of us and about 30–40 of them. Everyone brought their bottles out and started throwing them. When we ran out, we ran into them. I was getting bashed all over the place, but we chased and caught a few of them. We were stamping on their hands; we gave them a good hiding and headed back to the pub. Then the police turned up and it was like they had drafted in every available officer from all over Merseyside.

They came into the pub and started clattering some of the lads with their truncheons. Police and Blues were running everywhere. Fucking Tranmere were running everywhere! All you could hear was: 'You black bastards!' 'You niggers!' 'Get outside, get outside!' Then they just left us there.

We got into our cars and headed back to Birmingham city centre. After we got home, we went to a party at Edward's Number 8 bar. We had a chat about it. There were about 60 of us dressed in our Burberry and Aquascutum. We all looked the part – know what I mean?

* * *

At home, we had Arsenal in a midweek night game and we thought we would batter them senseless. Me and my boys had it with them before the match in a row that went on for 10–15 minutes; we ended up running for our lives around the Bull Ring, even though we'd ambushed them on the way from the station. We gave it to them but suddenly they put us on the back foot; I ended up running down the ramp and straight into a taxi.

I remember another time when we were uptown on a Saturday evening; Birmingham were playing Arsenal but I had no intention of going as I had no money. But we all gathered because we knew Arsenal were coming. There were about 15 of us hanging around by the train station. About 20 of them got off the train. We ran into them and *bang*, *bang*, *bang*! The police didn't want to know, so we got a few hits in and then we legged it. Sometimes, when you're fighting, you forget about the CCTV cameras.

CHAPTER FOUR

When we came out of being rude boys, we started to get into the jazz funk scene. On Sundays, they would have these all-dayers all over the country, in nightclubs that were open for the duration. I remember being in the Rock City in Nottingham, when this white lad came in dressed from head to toe in Burberry. He made the mistake of walking into the toilets and when he came out he had fuck-all on – he'd been taxed for the lot. That's what we went to these all-dayers for. Birmingham Townies put the fear of God into people. The head doorman would come up to me, saying, 'Please control your lads – we don't want no trouble in here tonight.'

We would take coaches to The Place in Stoke-on-Trent – me, Todd, Rupert, Kenyon, maybe 10 of us in all. We still went to football and a lot of these jazz funkers didn't like it, because we would bring trouble to The Place. At their all-dayer, we were all having a really good time, chatting up girls, laughing and joking. At the end of the day, we were sitting back on the coach, having a laugh, until it went off outside with all these London lads.

We immediately piled back off the coach and started running into these cockneys, giving it to them. All of a sudden, I felt a bash on the head – a brick had hit me square on the forehead, full force, and knocked me straight down on the floor. I got up with blood pouring from the gash on my head, wiped it off and started battling away. Some of the guys managed to pull me out of it and took me to the hospital, where I got stitched.

When I got back, I'd missed the coach, but one of the guys that took me to hospital in his car offered to take us back to Birmingham. After that, every time that Birmingham and London mixed in the same place there would be fights – even in clubs in different cities, like Rock City in Nottingham or Seventh Heaven in Doncaster. These all-dayers were just fighting, fighting, fighting – though I was also seeing women. I had my first child, Tara, when I was still in Birmingham at this time, as a teenager running around single.

We used to go to Wigan for the all-dayer scene, when they used to have the old jazz funk. We knew there were a few black lads there, but when we went to football I don't think they'd ever seen so many niggers landing in their town centre. There were 40–50 of us and we didn't know what we were coming up against. They knew who we were but we didn't know who *they* were.

We were walking around the town centre and we went to a few pubs, but we never got any trouble. We were getting plenty of looks though, as they'd never seen 40 black lads walking through their town centre. Even when we sat down in McDonald's, people were staring at us, though the girls were fine as to them we were just the fucking lads.

About a mile and a half away from the ground, we had it off with Wigan. It was nothing much but we thought we'd better show our presence. The police were quickly on the scene, they were watching our every move. It was just a quick off – *bang*, *bang*, *bang* and see ya later! We got in our cars and fucked off.

MAL

I lost track of him for a bit but I used to see him in town with all the rude boys; they used to kick in the doors. I met up with him and a couple of the other Zulu boys and he introduced me to them. We went to a club and this woman was having a go at one of the guys. One of the bouncers came over and he could see Barrington, because you could always see him standing above everyone, and he said to him, 'Don't get involved in this.' Barrington didn't kick off – but he could have.

I was brought up with Black Danny. I used to live in

Terrace Road and he lived on Villa Street, just around the corner from me, and we've known each other since we were six or seven years old. Black Danny was friends with a guy called Lloydy, one of Villa's main lads at the time, who is also my cousin. We've always been friends and, as we're related, we've never clashed.

I remember going to a match and seeing Black Danny, though we'd give each other a miss. We've had it off with Villa loads of times and always had to go looking for them. I remember a firm of us coming out of their ground, walking all the way around and there were no Villa in sight. We went down there looking for them, they didn't turn up and they tried to claim a fucking victory!

Villa were in the old First Division, now the Premiership, and we were always in the lower leagues during the mid-eighties, so we hadn't met for a long time. We've had it with West Brom and Wolves, but Villa are the main target. On one occasion that I remember, me, Todd, Rupert and about 15 of us met up in town and went to a pub in Broad Street. Half of us were in tracksuits. I always like to wear loose clothing so that I can punch, kick and run in them.

When we got to the boozer, the doorman said, 'Sorry, you can't come in wearing tracksuits.'

'You fucking what?'

'You can't come in wearing tracksuits.'

I pushed him out of the way and we walked into the pub.

Afterwards, we all got taxis down to Villa Park, but I missed all the fighting that went on down Rocky Lane. It was all organised and, as it was going off, people were getting phone calls saying, 'Get down 'ere, get down 'ere!'

Rocky Lane is the street in Aston where everyone arranged to have it off. There's a pub nearby and when we got there it was unbelievable. You could hear battle cries:

'ZULU!'

'C-Crew!'

Villa had outnumbered the Blues but we stood there and gave it to them. It was the sort of fight where nobody would run off, just like when we played West Ham. Apparently, there were police stood there with their handheld cameras. They had it so easy that day – I wish I'd been there, I'd have been lamping the police with their bloody cameras!

When the Blues played Villa at Birmingham one time, we were coming up from one of the boozers in Digbeth and we got a telephone call saying Villa were coming over the dual carriageway. So we all ran up to the top, where the pub is. There were about 200 lads up by the dual carriageway; somehow I made my way to the front of the firm. We were walking up and could see quite a few black lads coming down. All we heard was 'C-Crew, C-Crew!' Me, Brains, Rupert and Dougal all stood there. Up ahead I could see Black Danny, my cousin and another couple of lads I knew. We were heading away from Birmingham's ground, with Villa coming towards us. Everyone squared up, but then Villa took out baseball bats and knives. We just ran into them, though I bypassed Danny and my cousin.

Usually, when I see a tool being drawn, I back off – but I didn't want anyone to see me doing that. Dougal, who's a big fucker like me, was shouting, 'Come on! Come on!' There were now about 30 of us so we couldn't turn around and run, or we'd be running into ourselves. There were more of us, maybe two to one, but they were tooled up. I don't mind taking a beating off a bat but I don't want to get fucking stabbed!

As Lloyd and Danny ran past me, I kicked this geezer – then I backed off to the side. I did *not* want to get stabbed. All of a sudden, Dougal got banjo'd and I thought, *Fuck this, man!* Two minutes later, the police jumped in and it was: 'Thank fuck for that!'

When I saw Dougal, he was on the floor – completely spark-out. That's the point at which some fucking guy writes in Villa's book, 'The so-called famous Zulu cage fighter got knocked out.' I said to the guy who wrote it, 'If you think you KO'd me, come and have a square go at me then.' Black Danny knows it wasn't me who got knocked out.

Then the police turned up, so we picked up Dougal and went off to the match. I left the match with about 15 minutes to go and that's when we saw Villa coming towards us. They were black lads so we shouted,

'ZULU!' That's our war cry. All you could hear was 'ZUUULUUUUU!!!'

Then they started shouting 'C-Crew!' It was all of the old lads. All you heard around town after that was that we got done. And yeah – we did get done.

There's always talk of revenge but there's bigger fish to fry now. The history is there though. Even if you don't go to a match for five years, you still turn out for Villa/Blues. Not just for the fighting – you have to be there for the games themselves.

The trouble with derby matches is that all the guys come out of the woodwork. Blues don't go to England matches because they'd end up fighting with their own rival firms – we're not England, we're just Birmingham. We want the glory to ourselves. We don't want to say we joined up with Man U or blah-blah to beat fucking Slovakia or whatever.

I remember it was all in the news and the papers for about a week: 'The Blues came down Rocky Lane . . . X amount of people were arrested . . . X amount of police were injured.'

If I had to rate the top five firms, I'd say they were Cardiff, West Ham, Arsenal, Tottenham and Portsmouth. But, as far as the top firms we've personally come across, I'd say Villa, Leeds, West Ham and Cardiff, plus we've had some unexpected battles with fans in places like Wigan, Tranmere and Stoke.

Our group would always contain a mix of races: we

had black lads, white lads and Asian lads; we were a pretty multiracial bunch. When people go on about the Zulus being black, that's just something that outsiders instantly think or feel. Even the name 'Zulus' never came about until '82, when we played Man City and someone in our crowd shouted out, 'ZULU!' The name has stuck with us ever since.

With the Blues though, we do have a large black following and, when you go to certain away games, you see the team's fans thinking, *Look at them niggers down there, man!* They start shitting themselves and you think, *Fuck me, we've put the fear of God into 'em already!*

It's like when people look at me now. They judge me by appearance, but this can work to my benefit because, when I get into the ring and take my top off, the guy standing across from me thinks, *Fucking hell!* It's just a look, one moment when you know you've beaten that guy mentally already and you only need to go and do the physical stuff. By the time I go out there and raise my hands, he's cowering in the corner.

* * *

We'd always believed that West Ham were the top dogs, from everything we heard through the media. We'd have thought that Millwall were the worst, but we heard that West Ham gave it to them a couple of times. So everyone was teamed up to meet West Ham's so-called ICF.

Two weeks before the match, in Edward's Number 7 and 8 bars, all anybody would talk about was West Ham, West Ham, West Ham! ICF this and ICF that. Our firm had been together for around two to three years and we thought we were going to show that lot. We were the top dogs from the Midlands, but we wanted to be the top dogs in England.

A week before the match, we were all out shopping and getting our gear, shoplifting or breaking into a couple of shops. It didn't matter how expensive the clothes, you wanted the best clobber, the best shirt. On the day of the match, we met up in town; I was wearing a blue Pringle jumper, some cheap fucking stretch jeans and a Sergio Tacchini tracksuit top with the two stripes across the front.

About 9am, loads of West Ham came through the train station. We were at Edward's Number 8 bar, and as we got off the train there were around 20–30 of us mingling around town. Then we found a couple of West Ham outside a shop, so we fucking ran into them! Villa were away that day so we knew it was West Ham. They talk fucking funny anyway; you can tell them a mile off. We just fucking hammered them – there were bottles and glasses flying, girls and kids screaming and running. We all disappeared before the police turned up, back to the pub to sit down. We just chilled out for about 10 to 15 minutes, before one of the lads said, 'Let's make our way down to the ground.'

There were about 30 of us and we were all from different areas. As we walked down to the match, some of the West Ham fans had police escorts. We saw four or five black lads and automatically thought they were Brummies. We knew that West Ham were racist and played 'spot the nigger', so we went over to talk to them and found that some London teams had a few black lads running with them as well. We'd only previously heard of one black lad at West Ham, whose name was Cass Pennant.

We had a little row on the way down to the ground. Everyone was hyper, hyper, hyper! There was loads of Old Bill everywhere. We knew that West Ham would bring a firm because it was a cup match. Whoever was there were all fucking game!

We got to the match and stood behind the goals. There used to be a bit of waste ground behind the stand where we used to fight all the time. We used to call it the 'bomb peck' because it was full of bricks and debris. That was where we used to row with the police at the end of most matches and we had a couple of West Ham round there too, who we threw bricks at.

West Ham were at the other end, behind the other goal. We got into the ground and everyone was like, 'All right? All right, pal!' The place was packed, all you could see were West Ham and Blues flags, and everyone was jumping around.

A West Ham mob came running out on the pitch and we thought, *Fuck this!* Sitting behind the goal made it

BARRINGTON PATTERSON

easy to get on to the pitch, we only had to climb over one advertising barrier. People jumped out from everywhere and were trying to rip up the goalposts and seats. And then, all of a sudden, West Ham and Birmingham were clashing on the pitch. Bottles and chairs were flying everywhere.

Then the police came on to the pitch on their horses. They had truncheons and were beating people left, right and centre. Guys were dropping with split heads and there was blood all over the place. Both sides retreated but soon started fighting again; the police tried separating them but I think they only made it worse. They were just going around on their horses, knocking people over. This went on for some time.

One of the Blues managers came out and asked us to get back to our seats. We weren't going to though; we were giving it out to West Ham. I'd always wanted to fight and so here I was, but I'd never seen anything like it in my life. I was on the pitch and had my photo taken, turning up in an afternoon paper called the *Sports Argos*. In the picture I was holding a metal or wooden bar I'd just picked up off the floor, but I never got arrested for it.

Everyone got back in the stands now, shouting, 'Come on, let's get the bastards!' All the fans were getting together and the feeling was unbelievable! My heart was pumping 10 to the dozen and I was sweating like fuck. We just wanted to get outside. They'd come down to our manor so about 30 or 40 of us went outside to get them.

We got out into the courtyard behind the main Birmingham stand. We had to walk down the side of the ground, by some derelict houses that gave up a load of bricks. Everyone walked over to this bombsite to tool up with bricks and bottles. We grabbed slates and whatever else we could. The away fans hadn't got out yet, but we had little pockets of firms on every corner, waiting for them.

Then a firm-and-a-half turned up. West Ham were well organised and all you could hear was 'ICF! ICF!' I thought, *Fuck this!* Everyone had their bricks and bottles ready, so we just ran into them. But West Ham had some big fuckers and they stood on. We had a good ding-dong with them for around 10 to 15 minutes but guys were getting stamped on. I was fucking shitting myself! I was getting stamped on too, while other guys had cuts to their heads. People were screaming and crying – it was fucking proper, man!

I remember at one stage that a police officer got dragged off his horse and stamped on. It was a proper riot, unbelievable! The Old Bill never wanted to arrest anyone – they just wanted to batter you themselves. I guess they couldn't be bothered with all the paperwork, but they got a caning as well.

West Ham had a police escort so we backed off, but we always knew where it was going. We were in the backstreets, trying to pick off a few West Ham as they came past. We were throwing our bottles at them, trying to break through, but the police had them in a tight little escort. We couldn't really get at them and they couldn't get at us.

We went into town and had it off outside the train station again. Commuters were screaming and running, and taxis were trying to move out of the way so as not to get dented. All you could hear was 'ICF! ICF!' and '*ZULUUUUUUUUUUU!*' We knew we were with the big boys – but they were all men! It was like when we had Portsmouth, you weren't getting boys, these were big fuckers.

The police escorted West Ham through the train station. We waited for them for two or three hours, trying to pick off a few and give them a few slaps. My mate Sharky ended up taxing some London guy for a Tacchini top and a Burberry scarf. Happy days!

We went up into the Bull Ring after and had a little chat about the match, about what had happened and who'd got battered. We couldn't really believe that something like that had happened down at the Blues. We'd had it with West Ham toe to toe. They couldn't slag us off and we couldn't slag them, but at least we were rated. I think we got a bit of respect from West Ham for that day. I'd never seen anything like it.

* * *

When Pompey's 657 Crew came to town, there was just

me, Todd and Rupert, the lads I was always with. We'd just landed by New Street station and we didn't realise there was a football match on. Three fucking big lads walked up to us, asking, 'How do you get to the football ground?'

'That way.'

Then all you could hear was: 'We're Portsmouth!'

None of them were dressed like football casuals. One of them was wearing a green Harrington jacket and they all wore big working boots. *Who the fuck are you?* I thought. Todd went up and banged one of them and then one of them pulled a knife out. I thought, *I'm on police bail here, I don't really want to get involved.* There were plenty of police around and if I got arrested I'd be remanded in custody, so I just stood aside. Rupert started throwing punches and got slashed right across his hand.

They ran off and we got Rupert to the train station. The police took him to hospital. I know Pompey have got a fucking good firm, but I never actually got to meet them.

RUPERT & TODD

Rupert: *In those days, football was on a Tuesday and Wednesday, so all the fans would get a paper in the morning and I'd look and see who had to change at Birmingham. Because some of them did stop off and have a little walk around instead of changing trains, but after Man City and Everton it was like you came to Birmingham and then stayed on the other side of the* barrier; if you came to our side, it meant you wanted it. So we knew Portsmouth were coming in but we didn't know at what time. We used to have all these subways outside the train station, so we've seen 'em walk round the other way and intercepted them. They're at the bottom bit and they're all bunched up through weight of numbers; we had to back off a bit and they got one of the lads. They were saying, 'Come get your mate!' and they were proper geezers – the first time I'd really seen dressers, they had cowboy boots and everything on.

Todd: It was Portsmouth 657 but I remember it as just another bunch of blokes, because at that age we were constantly involved in violence and it was just another fight to me. The guys had said something about colour – 'Paki', 'nigger', whatever they were calling us – and I looked at Barrington, because I was always pretty lively myself, and I said, 'What you saying?' And Barrington said, 'Nah, nah, nah, I'm on licence.' And I said, 'I'm not being funny, Baz, if you're not going in, I'm not going in, simple.' Because I knew he'd got me covered. He's gone, 'Fuck it!' and just steamed in. They were blokes, we were kids and we were steaming 'em. We've all gone in and that day there were about seven of us fighting them on the stairs in the town gardens. They were getting knocked out like flies because all of us were active and up for it.

I've cracked one, and then Rupert's cracked him. As soon as he's done it, the blade's come out. I remember one of 'em pulled out a knife and nearly took Rupert's finger *off, so we've had to take him to the hospital to get it stitched back on!*

* * *

Leeds? What more can I say? A bunch of fucking racist bastards and they have been from day one! I've been up to Leeds a few times and it's 'nigger this' and 'nigger that'. It's not just Leeds but Yorkshire, and it's not just a black and white thing – they're racist if you're not from fucking Yorkshire!

The Leeds game was planned just like the West Ham one. All you used to hear back in those days was that Leeds had been away fighting in Europe. Most of the papers on the weekend were about Leeds, Leeds, Leeds! When we knew we had Leeds coming for a cup match, everyone was just fucking hyper, it was like we were having a party. Even a week before the match, everyone in town was talking about Leeds.

A couple of days before the match, we went out doing our dodgy stuff and earning a bit of poke. I think it was the season after the West Ham match. I was wearing a nice Burberry coat, a normal pair of jeans and probably a pair of Bjorn Borg trainers, which I used to love.

We all met up at McDonald's at the ramp, next to the fountain by the Bull Ring. There were about 20–30 of our little rude boy posse – my little firm. We were just happy that Leeds were coming to town. Then we all split up.

Some of the lads went down to the train station and, all of a sudden, a few Leeds supporters turned up – 10 lads here, 20 lads there. Fat Errol and a couple of lads were down the station and the police battered them with their truncheons. They dispersed the crowd as we just stood there watching.

We went back to Edward's Number 7 for a drink and a chat. All the spotters were out. Leeds turned up with a firm round by Edward's about 12.30 or 1pm. Then the police turned up and chased Leeds off. We couldn't do much because they kept us inside the pub.

A few of the lads caught a taxi down to the football ground. Me, Rupert, Todd and Big Chest Leroy joined about a dozen others to walk down to the match. We walked all the way through the Bull Ring and paid a little visit to the train station, but nothing happened down there. We headed down St Andrew's, which is the main street to the ground. Walking down, all you could see was a big fucking firm over the road and a police escort. Leeds were about 300-to-400-strong. So we stayed over the road as they clocked the 15–20 of us.

We were just walking normally down the street as the police came over and started whacking us with their truncheons. 'Move on! Move on!' We all had to split up as they were getting a bit heavy-handed. We didn't want to get arrested, we just wanted to have a good time at the match. I've been to a couple of matches where they made you go into the ground late, which is what the police did with Leeds. It fucks your head up really, because you pay all that money to go to the ground and end up getting in there 15–20 minutes late.

We stayed close together and watched the Leeds firm. There wasn't much they could do about it because the police escort was tight. Most of the time the police were busy watching us but they had their work cut out. All of a sudden, you got one or two bottles raining over from the Blues side. The police came over with dogs and chased us off; we ran off down some little side-streets and regrouped again.

We got into the ground right behind the goal, as usual. Leeds were up in the top left-hand corner. There was a row outside the ground and I think a wall came down. Then, all of a sudden, the burger van went up in flames! Inside the ground, Leeds started coming down onto the pitch so all the Blues ran onto it as well.

They had a big firm crammed into the corner of the ground where the wall came down. I remember running on to the pitch and getting out of breath – I wasn't very fit back then. Everyone got together like something out of *Braveheart*. When you stand there fighting, you get to find out who your friends are. If you're a black lad, you know when you're fighting a white lad; but we had a massive following of black and Asian lads at the time, and so you didn't know who was who at the end of the day.

We had it off on the pitch as the police came towards

us. Leeds retreated back to their end and the Blues continued coming forward. We were running them back and forth to their end for ages. The police managed to contain Leeds in their own half but we kept on coming. People were throwing things at the horses and trying to pull the police off them.

After the game, we heard on the radio that somebody had died after the wall collapsed. At the time we weren't bothered though – it wasn't a Blue, so we didn't really care. We were probably even fighting amongst ourselves, as there was no Leeds in our end. (I remember how, when we played West Ham, there were a few of them in with our fans.)

I think the Leeds fans ran on to the pitch to get away from the burger van on fire and the collapsing wall. So we just decided to run them on the pitch. It really kicked off – what a row! I was in my fucking element, man! I stood with a few of the lads as punches and kicks were thrown, like I was in some kung fu movie. People were getting dropped like flies.

I remember this white lad, a Blue, who stood back to back with a black lad and they were knocking out everyone in sight. Anyone who got in the way got banged, and after the game it happened again. All of us Blues lads went to the waste ground and the police came over. We started bricking them and chasing them off; they tried forming a line of riot shields but we gave it to 'em. We hammered them.

After 15–20 minutes, everyone disappeared and then walked back towards town. Some of us regrouped around the back of some houses in the backstreets, watching where the helicopter was. If you could see it, then you knew where the police were. We walked down the side-streets on the estates while Leeds walked past with the police. Bottles and bricks went raining over, anything that we could throw at them. The police chased us for a full half-mile and then we just walked back into town.

We waited round by the train station and, when Leeds arrived, it happened all over again. Everyone was running all over the place. One of the lads had some darts and he was throwing them at people. It kicked off outside the station and the police were chasing everyone with their truncheons before they got Leeds back inside.

A lot of people knew me because I was a name and I was always fighting around town – not just at football but on the club scene too. I was causing trouble, having it off with people; I made a name for myself slowly, gradually. When I first got into town I was just some guy from Handsworth. Then I started linking up with a group of lads from different areas, black lads, white lads and Asians. We were all out to do the same thing – earn some money.

* * *

Another time, we met up at New Street station for an away game at Leeds, about 30–40 lads – black, white and a few

Asian. Everyone was up for it, buzzing. We thought of getting off at the stop before Leeds and heading that way, but the police were waiting in heavy number, so we stayed on the train. They put us in an escort and it was the usual verbals – we were calling them 'scabs' and everything. Back then we still looked upon Leeds as a racist place, even though they had a small black community. The police held us up for half an hour on the platform, searching every one of us thoroughly before putting us on to waiting buses and moving us to a pub. There were the usual attempts to break the escort but the police weren't having any of it.

We knew they would turn up for the Blues, obviously having heard about our reputation. Nothing went on inside the ground. We were kept in for half an hour after the game and, as we came out, all you could hear was 'Leeds! Leeds! Leeds! We are Leeds!' and all that kind of shit. We were shouting, 'Scum! Scum!' as a few bottles came flying over. It didn't faze us. We thrived on the atmosphere of being surrounded by all these racists in yellow and white scarves, hundreds and hundreds of them. We didn't carry colours, we were dressers.

As the bricks and bottles were raining down on us, the police didn't do anything. But, as soon as we turned to have a go back at them, they took action and waded into us. We were basically caught in their ambush and just had to stay together as a pack. Some of us were breaking away to have a go, but we were getting stranded as too many of our own felt too threatened to back us up.

The police eventually got us back on the buses and away. When we got to the train station we'd had enough, as we felt the police were taking the piss out of us. So we set fire to the bins and used them as a barricade to push forward.

This resulted in a full-on scuffle with the police, until we got back on the platform and pushed back on to the train. Among ourselves the usual inquests started: 'We should have done this,' 'We should have done that.' Not for the first time, the call was that we were disorganised as a firm. A good few lads were hurting from the ambush or the lashing from the police. Between certain teams there will always be a history there. No one is going to forget what happened at Leeds, and this was always going to be their revenge for what happen at St Andrew's – when their fan died after a wall inside the ground collapsed.

CHAPTER FIVE

I moved to Coventry from Birmingham in 1987, after Coventry City won the FA Cup that year. I came over here for a weekend to see what it was like. Then I rang my mum and said, 'I ain't coming back.' I ended up staying here. I met a girl from Coventry called Alison, in Rock City, the Nottingham nightclub, and she later became my first wife. That's why I stayed. We got married; things were going fine. But later, even though I was married, I still wanted to be single; I was nightclubbing, shagging around.

At this time, there was a bit of a black and white thing going on in Coventry; it had a name as a racist area and you had blacks fighting whites. I'd first started working the doors when I was about 18 or 19 in Birmingham, for a guy called Glen. When I used to work the doors in

Birmingham, you could see the football politics and its effects. You would get guys from Manchester slip in, give it loads of sign language that they fancied something and then get clattered; they'd get drawn out and bashed up. We had a couple of Villa lads think that the Blues wouldn't notice them, but someone went, 'Look over there, that's so and so,' and the next thing you knew they were battered.

This was always going to happen to people coming from out of town on to the club scene in a city like Birmingham, with its vibrant nightlife. I can remember some real trouble when a few Arsenal got into a club and started trying to bully. Londoners are much like Americans – LOUD, they really do remind me of bigmouthed Americans, and it's not always the football lads.

For a couple of years, this served as my learning curve as to how things were run. When I moved to Coventry, I started doing things my way. I had an altercation at a nightclub where I went down to sort out this doorman. I was out with a friend called Froggy and we went to The Bull's Head in Binley Road, Coventry. Froggy went up to the bar and bought two drinks; he gave the girl behind the bar a £20 note – she only gave him back change for a tenner. So there was a big argument in the pub with the bar staff, then the manager came: 'I'm gonna get my doorman!'

I went out to the car, grabbed my baseball bat and whacked the manager. I walked out the pub and thought, *Fuck it! That's it, end of.*

About two weeks later, I was in the gym, just finishing my training session; I came out of the gym, took my training clothes off and got into the shower. About 10 or 15 minutes later, I came out and, all of a sudden, four big lads came in the gym. One of the lads, who I knew as Dave, put his hand across one of the cubicle doors and said, 'You come down my fuckin' pub again, there's gonna be trouble.'

So I'm thinking, *I'm stark bollock naked, there's four big lads 'ere – fair enough, mate, no problem.* I put my hands up and went, 'I'm sorry – I'll keep away from your pub.'

Then afterwards I got changed, didn't think anything of it and walked out – but for at least a month it kept playing on my mind. I was in town one Saturday and I thought, *Fuck it!* I walked up to a club called Studio 21 where this doorman was working. I went to the door and another doorman said, 'You're not coming in.'

''Ey, fuck you!' I pushed him out of the way and walked in.

It was a massive club and it was busy; I was standing behind a pillar. So obviously this doorman was radioing to the rest of the doormen: 'We've got some problems on the front door.'

They all came running towards the front door as I was hiding behind this pillar. The last doorman running was the guy I was after, so I've tapped him on the shoulder and said, 'So what are you saying now, mate?'

He just went *BAM!* Straight on my jaw!

I turned around and looked at him – he didn't drop me or anything – and went, 'Is that it, ya cunt?'

I grabbed him, got him on the floor, then mounted him and started raining down punches. I was punching him for about two minutes. Everybody was stood round watching when, all of a sudden, I felt a big kick to my jaw. I fell off him, got up and backed off a bit. This big fat guy they used to call Roberto pinned me against the bar with his big belly.

I can't move because this guy's 20-odd stone. So I'm reaching behind the bar, trying to grab something. I've managed to grab this ashtray; I'm just about to *whack* him on his head with it when someone's grabbed my hand: 'If you do that, you're gonna end up in prison for a long time.'

I now know that guy as Andre. Since that day 20-odd years ago, he's always been there. He's been there for my kickboxing career, and he's been there with me for nearly every fight I've fought, travelling the world with me as corner man in my fighting career. He's still my friend, my training partner and my works partner until this day. He's been like a brother to me and we went on to set up our own security firm: JAB UK – Johnny (who joined Andre on the doors when I was in prison), Andre and Barrington. I also had the honour of being Andre's best man in 2012.

They let me walk out; none of the doormen said

anything. Then I went into town, rounded up a couple of guys to come back to the club, and this was probably about one o'clock in the morning. By the time we got back to the club, it was closed down – all the doors were shut! But the doorman was in hospital for about two weeks; he was pleading: 'Please, I don't want no trouble!'

It's mad how things pan out. Jez, the gaffer of the bar who I had the hump with over Froggy's change incident, turned out to be a good mate of mine; we often laugh about it.

ANDRE

I met Baz about 25 years ago and I can sum him up in a number of ways: he is a best mate that would stand his ground for you, no matter what; he is loyal – if he is your friend, then he's a friend for life; he is really funny and he is fiercely protective of his family and close friends. He is like a brother to me. And he is naughty – but nice!

I met Baz in a bizarre situation really. I was acting as a peacemaker between him and another doorman I was working with at the time. He and Baz had come to blows and I was asked to try to sort it out. So a meeting was arranged and I was told to go to Baz's house. At the time, me and him were only on speaking terms, not mates, so as you can imagine it was like going into the lion's den. Could he turn on me? Could this go wrong?

Cutting a long story short, Baz was reasonable, the issue was sorted and we agreed to meet up the next week and go out for a drink together. From that first night out, we became like brothers and we were out every weekend together: Baz and Andre.

* * *

The first club that I got on the doors with Andre in Coventry was in an area called Cheylesmore. Reflections was the roughest place in town. At the time, it was the main club in town where all the locals came to do their drug deals and link up, and it was frequented by a lot of lads, faces and dealers. It was the kind of place where the birds were like the blokes – glassing each other.

I approached it by offering them respect: I had to do my thing when I was there at night-time and they could do whatever they did in the day – smoke weed, etc. But if I and my team were working, they were going to have to be more discreet about it than they had before.

I was grafting five or six nights a week there, earning good dough. One night, I was standing on the front door and this guy came running out of the club, covered in claret. He was in a rush to leave so I'm thinking, *He's glassed someone.*

I chased after him and bashed his head off for causing shit on my door. It transpired he had stabbed two guys.

Every other night, it was the same in there. I was banging people out left, right and centre. I really had to earn my dough. That's where I made my stamp and got my reputation. At the time, gun crime was rife in Coventry; it's never been my thing and I would rather have a straightener. But I was standing in the club one night, talking to a friend, and someone walked in and shot the guy standing behind me. That's just how they went about things.

As time went on, my reputation built up in Coventry and I was getting offered top dough to sort out troubled clubs and bars. But it was blacks versus whites and there I was in the middle, because I'm a Brummie. I couldn't get on with the black guys because I'm from Birmingham and the white guys didn't like me because I'm black *and* from Birmingham.

I also remember working the doors when about five coach-loads of Londoners arrived for this big R&B event being held in the club and it was, 'We're from Sarf London,' we're this and we're that. I said, 'Fuck you, you're on my fucking manor and you're not in London now, you fuckin' cunts!'

I had a couple of good doormen from Birmingham working with me and I can tell you that the Londoners got a fucking hammering. They had to jump back on their coaches and fuck off.

I did have two lads from Coventry working with me inside, but at Reflections I found myself working most nights of the week and fighting every one of those nights to earn my status. I can recall, on a Friday night, fighting six or seven men at once out on the street. I'd be fighting black lads and I'd be fighting white lads, then the black lads would be fighting the white lads and I'd just let them get on with it. As long as it was not inside my club, I'd let them deal with each other.

It wasn't easy working as a team on the door, as I was an individual and also a bit madder than the others. There were a couple of times I needed a bit of help and had to go over to Birmingham to get a couple of lads to come down for me, as the Coventry lads couldn't be relied on. You've got to take into account that this wasn't my own team, but I'd hear things like: 'Oh, they know where I live,' or 'I'm not getting involved because they'll be around my house.'

Fuck that, man, I need you to stand with me!

I did that for years, working with guys I couldn't rely on until I started making some good friends I could trust with my back. But it was a tough club to work; I've experienced guys driving through the door in a car at me; I've seen shootings in there, I've seen two guys stabbed to death. This is the club I showed Danny Dyer when he was making his *Deadliest Men* programme; you could say it's a place with a history.

ANDRE

At this time, Baz and I were both working on the doors at different venues in Coventry. Trust me, the late eighties in Coventry on the door was hard work; most nights you would be fighting. As time went by and after a lot of talking, me and Baz started working together. This was the turning point when we started our own company; it was hard work to begin with but we started getting a lot of contracts so things soon looked good. Baz used to say, 'You're the brains, I am the brawn.'

The funny thing was we were getting all the shithole pubs in Coventry that no other companies wanted as they couldn't manage the clientele that went in these places. But at this time we turned nothing down, and whenever we got a new door me and Baz would go to work it until we cleaned the place up. Then we would put guys in and move on.

There were lots of fights and Baz would NEVER take shit or back down – it's just not his style. On one particular occasion, there was a guy who came to the door and you could just tell he was a cock straight away (and we had a saying: if you let shit in, then you will have to deal with it, so don't let it in). I turned him away. He walked off but within two minutes he had picked a fight with an innocent guy (I told you he was a cock) who didn't want to know. So Baz, who hates bullies, went outside the pub and shouted to him to leave the guy alone. This bully made a massive mistake because he pulled out a knife, turned round to Baz and shouted, 'Fuck off, you black bastard! Do you want some of this?' He was waving his blade.

Before this guy had a chance to say anything else, Baz was running towards him. His face showed complete shock: he was looking at the knife, back at Baz, back at the knife. (He must have been thinking, What the fuck? Who is this fucking nutter? I have the knife, not him!) Baz was getting closer and 18 stone of muscle running at you is quite scary. This bully got on his heels but Baz is fast for the first 200 metres (if he's not caught you by then, you may get away).

The guy ran around a bus and back towards the pub. At this point, I stepped back into the doorway till he ran past and swept his feet. Let's just say the bully got what he deserved. I don't think he'd ever do anything like that again.

Not many people get to know how funny Baz is. Trust me, his sense of humour is second to none and he never misses an opportunity to take the piss out of anyone in his company. On one occasion, I was working with him, he was on the door and I was inside. Yes, it kicks off and I am fighting with a lot of people. To cut a long story short: by the time Baz finally got there it was all over. I had a nice new red shirt instead of my nice fresh white one.

I said to him, 'Where the fuck was you?'

Baz said, 'Is that your blood on your shirt?'

I said no, so he laughed and said, 'All this sparring we've been doing has paid off then. I trained you well – that's my boy!' Then he went back to the bird he had been chatting to.

CHAPTER SIX

It wasn't until I worked in Coventry in the late 1980s that my kickboxing actually started. At this time, I was still trying to combine my bodybuilding with kickboxing. One was helping me with the other: I was the guy with one eye smaller than the other who looked like the Incredible Hulk.

I used to be reasonably good at art at school and I used to sit drawing these muscleman figures. It wasn't until after I left school that I started training at a Community Centre in Birmingham with one of my close friends at the time, Charles Gappa. When we first started, there were these two brothers in Newtown who were training there; they were pretty big and I always wanted to be as big as them. So we used to train hard there about four or five times a week.

I was about 18/19 at the time. I trained for a couple of years and then I found out what they were taking to get big; so I started taking the same thing: steroids.

I was always into my martial arts, and I was one of those guys who responded well to the training I was doing. About '86/'87, I started doing my first bodybuilding shows and I knew I looked good. But guys who came first, second and third were on more gear – or 'bigger' gear – than I was taking. I wouldn't take a jab. These guys would say, 'You need to start taking this/that so you can get bigger,' but I wouldn't because I was always shit-scared of needles.

But I got into it. I carried on training; I was downing more tablets and getting bigger and bigger. My first thought was always for my martial arts and, as I was getting more into bodybuilding, I was finding it difficult to walk because my legs were getting so big. I actually had to walk around with talcum powder because I was getting sores between my legs.

I carried on doing kickboxing and bodybuilding at the same time, and then the guy I was training with entered a competition. There was always banter between me and Charlie about who was better and we both entered for Mr Birmingham. He was taller than me and I always thought he looked better than me, but on the day I beat him and he's never lived it down. (He came second and a lad called Terry White came third.)

I had abs all the year round, so I never had to diet for

a show. I had a fast metabolism so I was one of the lucky ones; I never had to do anything. I went to quite a few bodybuilding shows and I've won a few: Mr Birmingham in 1988; Mr East Anglia in Great Yarmouth, 1988 and 1989. One Friday, I was in the gym training and I needed some money; I was running short. There was a competition on the Sunday so I went there, entered it and won the £500 first-prize money. I even entered a show last year in Coventry for the over-40s and came second.

I enjoyed the competitions, but now that I'm getting a bit older my metabolism's slowing down. You've got to get into the diet part, which I'm not really keen on, but I still enjoy the bodybuilding. It's not just posing; there's an art to bodybuilding as well, just like there is to fighting.

When I first started I did it to pull girls, I did it to stand on the door – plus I did it to fight as well. You've got a lot of guys who are bodybuilders and stand on the door, but they can't fight fucking sleep. So I did it for all those reasons but my interest in sport was always martial arts. The bodybuilding was to make me look good for the martial arts, as well as showing me how to look after my body. I want to be able to walk down the street or walk on the beach and stand out a mile off.

When I've gone in the ring and taken my shirt off, sometimes I didn't even need to throw a punch. Guys would just look at me and start shitting themselves.

I joined Dev Barrett's club in 1989, when I'd just got out of bodybuilding and wanted to get into kickboxing.

DEV

In 1971, I was introduced to the martial arts by a friend called John Johnson. There was no such thing as kickboxing then; we practised a style called shotokan karate at the Longford skating rink in Coventry and we had two amazing martial artists as instructors: Mick and Rick Jackson. I stayed loyal to that style, to that club and to those instructors for many years. The only time I did anything different was when I worked as a contract electrician and often travelled to many different cities up and down the country. At these times I would join the best martial arts club in that city, so I had a chance to experience training in taekwondo in Oxford, shotokan in Leeds, wado ryu in Swindon, kyokushinkai in Bridgend and kung fu in Swansea. But I always looked forward to coming back to the rink.

When Barrington turned up at my gym in the late 1980s, I at first thought he was one of these people who caused some trouble the week before, when I was away; I was expecting to hear something from them. I didn't think Barrington and this guy John were going to stick out the training; I was quite confused about what they were doing there.

Barrington trained really well and he did show ability, but he was just so much of a bodybuilder at the time. He'd just won a Mr Birmingham competition so he was really defined when he came to me. He loved his weights as well and in the back of my mind I was thinking, What do you want? *I was thinking of explaining my situation with rugby: I was also doing boxing, karate and full contact at the same time too. But you have to make a decision. If you want to make it to the top in something, you can't do everything, then you'd just be a jack of all trades.*

We were obviously doing the regular training and I always encourage people to train for competition and self-defence, but first to learn the basics and then go on towards the fighting. Barrington started off that way. Whenever he was training, obviously he was just interested in the main thing: fights. But you have to do conditioning, like flexibility. So when we'd exercise we'd always hear him crack some smartarse thing like: 'Are we doing fucking ballet then?' I'd say, 'Listen, I'm not joking, if you carry on doing that sort of thing, you'll be out of the class!' I remember one time we were exercising and I said, 'OK, legs apart!' And then he turned to this girl training beside him: 'You should be used to that, shouldn't you?' She looked at him and said, 'Fuck off!' But he was always like that. You could never teach a serious class when Barrington was around, he knew how far to push but would never go too far. Classes were quite fun sometimes though – he took the seriousness out of the class.

When Barrington had a big fight coming up, we would sometimes go to Bedford to spar with Matt Skelton, and to find someone who could actually push him around was an eye-opener. I wasn't surprised because I knew that, when he was at that level, no matter how big and how strong Barrington was, Matt would have the advantage because of his experience; he was an amazing Thai boxer. He was a big fellow but a real athlete as well. He went on to box pro as British and European champion, and he was a tough fighter.

We went to a tournament featuring one of my fighters and I invited Barrington along to see how he did. They were short of a fighter – somebody didn't turn up, one opponent pulled out – so they were asking if there was a heavyweight around that would take the fight on. So of course Barrington got up, and I think that was where it started. I think he was probably about an orange belt then. With us the belt sequence is red, white, yellow, orange, green, purple, blue, brown and black. At that time, I would have thought he'd been training for up to a year. When he fought for the first time, it was against Clive Tennant's student. Clive was one of my students but he now had his own club in Rugby; he was one of my first black belts and he actually made it to number-two Light Heavyweight in the country at karate and kickboxing. He also fought for a British title – but he lost.

One Sunday night in 1990, we went to a show at the Tower Ballroom, Edgbaston. Me and a couple of the lads drove down there and there were a couple of lads from our club in Coventry down there too. I think it was about a tenner to get in.

After about three or four fights, the announcer came in the ring and said, 'There's a guy here who has trained really hard for his fight and his opponent hasn't turned up. Is there anybody who would like to fight him?'

I thought, *What?* 'Yeah, I'll fight him!'

This guy was a big fat fucking lump! I didn't ask about getting paid, I just wanted to fight. My trainer said, 'Yeah, fight if you want.'

I'd made no preparation but I looked at the guy and thought, *You fucking fat cunt! Damn right I'll give it a go!* I had no kit on me but there was a stall selling fighting gear. The promoter got me a pair of shorts and a gum shield; I ran into the kitchen and boiled the shield in the kettle. I was given a box for my groin too.

I went to the changing room and had a 10- to 15-minute warm-up, then put on my long trousers and box. I got bandaged up and came out. Nobody was cheering for me because nobody had expected me to be fighting – including me; I'd just gone there to watch. I felt really nervous as this was my first time. I was shitting myself really.

As I said, the guy I was fighting was a big fat lump. I was 16 stone at the time, aged 24–25, and he was a bit older than me. But he was huge! My corner said, 'Come on, Baz, you can do it!'

'I'll give it a bash!'

I came out for the first round and it was *jab, jab, jab*. It was two-minute rounds and I thought, *Yeah, nice and easy, I'm ready for this.* I got in there and in the first round I had my guard up.

Then my head went back and I thought, *Fucking hell!* The very first kick he tried, he ended up ripping his fucking shorts! He was obviously so fat that he couldn't wear long trousers. I jumped on him and I was like *bang! Bang! Bang! Kick! Kick! Kick!* I thought, *I'm not even touching the fucker! I'm hitting him as hard as I can and it's not even affecting him.*

There were too many rounds. I was unprepared for it and I was just completely fucking dying. I was only used to fighting on the streets and knocking everybody out with one punch, but when you're in the ring and you've got gloves on it's totally different. He was fat and when I was hitting him I was just bouncing off him.

DEV

In the first round, I thought he was just headhunting and I said to him, 'Go for the body,' and I remember him throwing punches into the body. Barrington didn't take his training so seriously, he took it very light-heartedly but he still managed to do things. I think that was probably one of the things that made me think, Yeah, he could be good, and now he's going to fight. I know the impact it'll have on him because I know the difference between fighting in the streets and fighting in the ring. *I actually knew what was going to happen to him. I knew he was going to feel like his arms were going to pop and I knew the burning pain he was going to feel. I said to Barrington before the fight, 'This guy has obviously trained for the fight and you haven't. You are big and strong but fighting a skilled fighter is different to football hooligans.'*

He's still the same now, but I always advised him to be careful. He just says, 'It's all right, it's all right.' He has an attitude which is great really – he's just so positive. If ever I was away and needed a class covered, I could just ring him and he'd be there. Ninety per cent of the time he is like: 'Where? When? I'll be there.' You'd phone him and say, 'There's a guy fighting tonight.' 'Where? When?' He's just so good in that way – absolutely amazing!

So he plastered this guy not because he was big and strong, but because of his approach to the fight. I didn't really look for ambition in Barrington before, but after that fight I thought, Wow! I didn't have to look for it now – it hit me in the face. I thought he could definitely go somewhere and I was getting phone calls left, right and centre. People wanted to fight him.

I backed off and then came forward again. He was so fucking fat that he wasn't even feeling it. I was punching and kicking but I was out of breath already. It was only the first round and I was panting like fuck! He grabbed on to me and I grabbed on to him. I thought, *I ain't letting go of you, ya bastard!*

He's trying to work me, to punch and kick me, on the inside. I'm just grabbing on for dear life. Now it's the end of the first round and I'm back in my corner. I say, 'Fucking hell, Dev! What am I doing?'

'Come on, Barrington,' he says, while throwing water over me, 'you can do it. There's only four minutes left.'

That was the longest two minutes ever. When you're in the gym sparring, it goes just like that, but this was the longest two minutes I've ever done.

Next thing the bell went. I came out. *Bang, bang!* He jabbed me in my face and winded me in my stomach. He nearly fucking dropped me. I looked at my trainer and said, 'I'm all right, Dev, I'm all right.'

'Come on, get your hands up, work off the jab!'

Every time I went forward, the guy was knocking me into the corner or the ropes. I just stood there playing with him for a bit. At the end of the second round, I went back to my corner and dropped on the stool. I reached my hands back to support myself and Dev said, 'Get your hands off the ropes!' He stretched my legs out and started massaging them, threw water on me and said, 'Come on, you can do it. You *can* do it!'

'I've had enough, man.'

'Barrington, you've only got two minutes left!'

I thought I'd done eight minutes already – it had been the longest four minutes of my life. I managed to get myself together and come back out, but within the first 10 to 15 seconds of the round I was burnt out. The guy was hitting me and I was letting him carry on. I thought, *I hope he fucking burns himself out!*

Then, in the last 15 seconds, I went *bang, bang, bang, bang!* I threw about five or six punches. It was the end of the third round so I went back to my corner and Dev threw some water over my neck. I was out of breath, asking him, 'What happened, Dev?'

Then all I heard was: 'And the winner is Barrington Patterson!'

I couldn't believe it! I'd just won my first fight. It was the hardest six minutes of my life and I never wanted to do another one. But Dev said, 'Well done! We'll try and get you back in the ring to fight again.'

It got easier after that. I just went with it from there on.

I won the fight –
as you can see!

Above: Just married: Tracey and I are photographed between my mum, Dorothy (left), and my step-mum, Colleen (right).

Below: I have a sister in New York: Joy is pictured (centre) with her family.

Right: Me, Todd, Sharkey and the boys (left-right) were all Townies.

Left: My mate Bajey and me out with the lads during the mid-eighties, at the Power House in Hurst Street.

Right: Flexing to impress the ladies.

Bodybuilding made me look good for the martial arts – as well as teaching me how to look after my body.

Inset: Mr Birmingham 1988.

Left: My first K-1 fight victory against Shaun Johnson in 2000 at Aston Villa leisure centre.

Right: In 1995 I was crowned W.A.K.O. British Champion – for the fifth year in a row.

Left: Working my hands on a punch bag, which I also use to practise my kick.

Left: I couldn't walk down the road without the locals asking for autographs or a photo

Right: As you can see, I was in great shape here – photographed with my trainer and manager, Dev, plus one of the locals.

Left: At Waikiki Beach, all I could see was my picture and my name in lights on those big billboards: 'Dennis Alexio vs. Barrington Patterson for the IKF World Heavyweight Championship'.

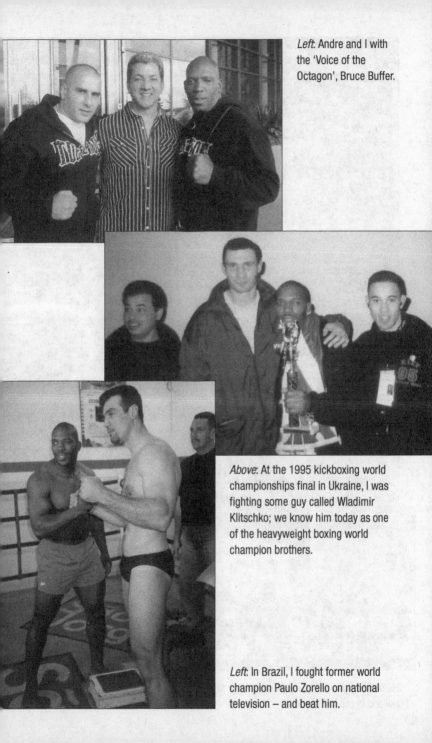

Left: Andre and I with the 'Voice of the Octagon', Bruce Buffer.

Above: At the 1995 kickboxing world championships final in Ukraine, I was fighting some guy called Wladimir Klitschko; we know him today as one of the heavyweight boxing world champion brothers.

Left: In Brazil, I fought former world champion Paulo Zorello on national television – and beat him.

Vrij was fighting in memory of his dad who died from cancer; I was fighting just because it was a fight.

Left: Dick Vrij was a hard bastard to fight, a real lunatic.

Right: The Coventry posse all came over to Holland in support of me.

CHAPTER SEVEN

I trained for about a year before my next fight. I fought a guy from Wolverhampton, a big Rasta called Victor Gayle. A big fucking dread man! This was for the Midland Area Title so I asked my mum to come and watch, though she'd said she never wanted to see me fight.

It was at the Molineux Centre by the football ground. When I clapped eyes on him, I thought, *Fuck me! He's a big lump of a lad! I'm gonna have my work cut out 'ere.* The atmosphere was unbelievable – at least 400 people were there. I'd got there a couple of hours before the fight and sat in the changing room, just cracking jokes with my mates.

My mum and sisters were there so I went over to see them. Then I went back to the changing room, got changed and warmed up. Whenever I get nervous, I go to the toilet all of the time; even though I never piss, I stand there with my dick in my hand but can't go. It's just the adrenaline.

There were two more fights before mine so I warmed up and got into a little sweat. I felt good as I knew that I'd trained hard for this fight, although I also thought it was going to be really hard as he was such a big lump. But, in the event, he never had anything to offer me really.

I walked out to my music playing: 'Walk like a Champion' by Buju Banton, the song that's been played throughout my whole career. Gayle came out second because he was on his home turf. Everyone was jumping up and down, clapping him. I came out in the first round and just hit and moved – hit and moved – kicked and moved. He never threw anything back. I stuck a couple of jabs into his face and he was cowering down in the corner. I gave him a couple of kicks too, and then, all of a sudden, he came out and threw this wild punch on my jaw. It threw me back on to the ropes; I bounced back off and shook my head, thinking, *Fucking hell!* That was the end of the first round.

I went back to the corner and Dev said, 'Keep your guard up. If that had caught you, you'd have been knocked out.'

I said, 'Don't worry. I know what I gotta do.'

It was a five-round fight. I went back out there – jab, jab – left hook – dropped him on his arse. When he landed on the canvas, it was like *boom!* The guy fell into the ropes and tried to get back up. By this time, I was thinking, *Please don't get up. I don't want any more – I'm tired!* Even though I trained hard for the fight and the adrenaline was pumping, I just didn't want to do any more. He crawled up to the ref and the ref said, 'Carry on fighting.'

DEV

He would have got a count of eight and the referee would have said something like, 'Can you hold your hand up?' Sometimes they push your hand and if your balance is poor, then you're obviously unable to continue. Sometimes they'll just say, 'Put your hand up!' and if you put your hand up they'll say it's OK.

I just jumped on him: *bang, bang* – kick, punch – kick, punch. The referee jumped in and stopped the fight. I thought, *Fucking nice one!* My mum came over and I gave her a kiss, but she said, 'I'm never coming to watch you fight again.' Even though I've had loads of fights since, she's never been to another.

When I got my belt on, I was so proud to have won the Midland Area Title. Then I got offers to fight, fight, fight. About a year after I had my first fight, I had one in Barnsley – but a couple more had happened before that. Basically, everyone there was white. In those days, Barnsley was a really racist area and I was fighting the Barnsley area champion. They were saying, 'Look at the size of that fucking nigger!' and things like that. It was at that fight in Barnsley that they were calling my wife a 'fucking nigger lover'.

RUPERT

He's fighting in this ring and when Barrington fights he's an entertainer, so you'll hit him and his legs will go but you know he's entertaining the crowd. So he's fighting and there's this table full of lads who are really loud and giving Barrington loads of shit during the fight. Barrington's keeping this lad up really, as he isn't in his class, and next thing it's BANG! He's knocked the lad out and then got straight out the ring, gone up to them and said, 'Who the fuck wants it?' That's Barrington!

They were all racists, man. We had another one when he went to Barnsley and they were all going, 'You black bastard!' He knocked out their local champion. Barrington used to become an angry, angry man when he heard stuff like that. He used to say, 'Them days are gone, man, them days are gone!'

After about five years married to Alison, the marriage wasn't working out. Alison had given me my second child, whose name is Leonie. But I was cock happy; I started shagging round here, shagging round there. She found out about it and we split up, and with this I met my second wife.

I was seeing another girl at the same time, called Linda.

We had a little baby girl called Bailey, who's 18 years old now; I ended up getting married to Linda, which was a big mistake.

Around this time, there were summer fights in Holland so I went over there for a couple. That was how I made my name in Holland in the late eighties and early nineties, when kickboxing was big over there. I always wanted to be World Champion of the sport.

DEV

We started to do the international circuit. Barrington is just one of those people who draws other people towards him. He is like a magnet. It doesn't matter where someone is from, they can be from anywhere from Russia to Brazil or most European countries – he always has the crowd on his side. He is an entertainer and he's never boring. I actually refused a lot of fighters in this country because of the problems it may cause. When he fights, he's not cocky or bigheaded but he does like to mess about a bit. He does his showboating but is very gracious when it comes to winning or losing. Especially when he loses – he just takes it.

One of the cleanest knockouts I've ever seen Barrington do was this guy from Rotterdam; he'd bought a coach-load with him who were supposed to be National Front-type people. He's got to be 140 kilos; he's tall, wide, like a barrel chest and belly all in one. Barrington hit left to the body, right over the top. It was like in a movie when someone's unconscious but standing and he doesn't fall. This is no exaggeration at all: when he hit the canvas it was like the whole room shook, and he was out. Of course, Barrington does his showboating as well: messing about, dancing around the ring, the 'Ali shuffle'. Sometimes he would look at the guy at that point – but always, at the end, he would go and shake his hand and be really respectful. It was just that 30 seconds of showboating.

The people of Northern Holland had adopted Barrington as one of theirs; they were so happy because he'd beaten somebody from Rotterdam. So, of course, after the fight we were told the local Rotterdam people were all waiting outside for Barrington, because they didn't like what he'd done or his showboating either. So they had to lock us in the changing room and I'm talking about long after the show had finished, because they were going to come back in as well. We wouldn't go outside, obviously – though he wanted to! We had to wait there until everybody had gone.

When you're a good street fighter, you think you can just put some gloves on and knock someone out. At first, I was hungry and just wanted to fight, to make a name for myself and earn my status. I was training with a lot of boxers and, if it hadn't been for my eye injury, I think I could have become a traditional boxer. I was sparring with guys like cruiserweight champion Rob Norton and various others who were good boxers. I was holding my own against them, so if I'd had good vision in both eyes I think I would probably have gone into boxing. (I used to spar with Matt Skelton, a heavyweight kickboxer who kicked like a mule and also carved out a boxing career.) I've never regarded myself as being blind in one eye. I was ducking, diving and blocking punches, doing everything that a guy with two eyes could do – probably doing it better.

Throughout my career, I've only been knocked out once and that was in an MMA fight. Having the disadvantage of one eye has made me the person who I am today. So, to any other guys with one eye, or even only one leg – just fucking go for it, man!

CHAPTER EIGHT

In 1988/89, when me and this lad from Birmingham were still working on the club door at Reflections, I got to meet a couple of the lads from Coventry – including one called Fatty Smith who I'd known from when I did six months in Whatton Detention Centre in Nottinghamshire in my teens. (It was like a fucking army camp in there.)

The rave scene had just started kicking in then, and I think every known troublemaker was frequenting the place I was working at. I was working with Bulldog, Big Del and a couple of others – all known lads in Coventry, though I'd not known them that long and didn't know how much I could trust them.

There was one particular incident when I was standing on the door, in my bowtie and all that, when I had to rush inside to where this guy was hitting his girl. I said, 'Come on, mate, leave it out, will yer?' He turned round and swung for me, so I banged him one and he slumped against the fruit machine, then he fell on the floor. Me and the other doorman managed to get him up and shoved him outside, then closed the door.

I didn't think any more of it as we stood there, chatting to the receptionist and the other guys on the door. We had two cameras on the road outside, so you could see who was coming to the door.

All of a sudden, we felt this big shudder. I jumped back and looked up at the camera to see this fucking guy had driven his car through the front door. The car had mounted the pavement and crashed through the club's entrance. A couple of our doormen went out the back door and round to the front, and dragged him out of the car. We gave him a beating until the police came.

Reflections was really busy, as we used to get firms of lads all the time looking to start trouble. You'd get lads from Bell Green who would be fighting lads from Wood End; guys from Tile Hill would be fighting guys from Canley, and so on. One particular night, the DJ stopped the music, which was a sure sign of trouble, so we all ran towards the dance-floor area to where the DJ's view would have been. We found two guys had been stabbed, one in the groin. We managed to get them outside on to the pavement but, tragically, both guys bled to death in front of a big crowd of onlookers. By the time the police came, they could only seal off the road with tape and start a murder inquiry. It was a violent period, as only weeks before the club's head doorman had got stabbed to death in an incident outside the nightclub.

A year after that, I was right in front of a guy who got shot in the leg on the dance-floor. Some of what I experienced working there seems unbelievable now. Another night, I got waylaid by about 10 police officers outside the club and ended up in court for it – where they threw the case out, rightly, as I'd done nothing. I'd just got jumped.

I did get banged up for a few months for another offence, so I had to be away from the door and leave it to Andre. By the time I came out, he had got together with this guy Johnny. It worked out well between us all and we became known as 'JAB'. We were starting to get offered more doors. This was the early nineties, and, befitting the times, we were doing a lot of raves, one-off events that paid serious money.

TODD

I remember Barrington once invited me over to Coventry to the big pub he worked in, not far from where Rupert used to live. I think it was The Red Lion. It was pretty rough; Barrington was doing what he was doing and I was having a drink. Two lads started fighting pretty bad; one of them was knocked out on the floor and Barrington looked at me, smiled and said, 'Watch this.'

And he got this boy by the bollocks and neck; he was a big lad and he dead-lifted him out of the pub. Barrington, being Barrington, was pushing his chest out and feeling all good about it. He must have chucked this geezer a good 15 feet. Barrington just smiled at me and went back to his work. I thought, Some things never change! *That's typical Barrington. That would have been around '91. Then there was another guy, a big black geezer as well, who must have been about six foot five and he was always giving it the big 'un to Barrington. Barrington's gone up to him and given him a roundhouse; Barrington can only be about five foot ten and a half because he's the same size as me, but he knocked him out by fly-kicking him in the mouth.*

* * *

In May 1993, my brother Eric was staying with me in Coventry due to the breakdown of the relationship with his children's mum. I knew he was going through some shit at the time, but I never dreamt what the outcome would be that morning when he left for work.

That evening, he didn't come home. I just thought, *He's made it up with his missus and it's all sorted out.*

Then I got a call from my mum. I will never forget her words: 'You need to come home. Eric has killed himself.'

Those words cut me to the bone more than anything in my life.

I had to be strong for my family and hold them together. I never show emotion – it's a sign of weakness.

I say what I have to say when I visit his grave; he was the only brother I knew and grew up with, so when he went a part of me went too. Eric left behind three young children; shortly after, they moved away with their mum.

Twelve years later, I got a message saying that a young lad was looking for me and that I was his uncle. It was Eric's son, Cameron. I was buzzing when we met up at New Street, Birmingham. We talked about his dad and the things we got up to as youngsters on the streets.

Cameron didn't really remember his dad, so I filled in the gaps. I was hurt when he said that his mum had changed their name from Patterson; it really bothered me how some people can be so cruel, though, of course, she may have had her own reasons.

I will always be a part of Cameron's life. Having him back in my life is like having a part of my bro back.

* * *

In the mid-nineties, I was working at the Ministry of Sound, near the Elephant & Castle in south London. They used to have 15 lads from Birmingham go up there every Friday and Saturday. We were working for an Asian guy called Peely in London: me, my mate Clayton and a couple of lads working on the main doors, a load of guys from out of town working with their people.

The main guy who ran the door would be like a spotter, spotting the London guys who were troublemakers; he'd say to us, 'No, he can't come in.' What they wanted was for guys from outside town to front them up; London guys wouldn't front them because they were pals. It's just like some clubs around Coventry: they put guys from Birmingham on the doors and put the Coventry guys inside. A lot of places do this: they don't want to put their guys on the door; they'd rather have guys from out of town working. I used to work at a club down in Watford as well – it was the same thing. We used to get a load of Londoners coming up, causing trouble.

They had probably about 20-odd doormen at the Ministry of Sound because it was a big place, it was so busy. They used to have some big barriers along where you went to get in. I was off the main door and I remember this mixed-race kid, quite smartly dressed, with a group of white kids and black lads; he was going 'bloodclaat this' and 'bumbaclaat that'. I have a laugh and a joke with everyone, so I turned round to him and said, 'What you talking like that for, mate? You're not even black.'

Everyone burst out laughing – even his friends! I was just seeing it as a joke but this guy turned round and said, 'You pussy'oles from Birmingham! I'm gonna take a Birmingham man out, I'm gonna shoot ya!'

'Yeah, fuck off, ya twat! You think you're gonna shoot me? Fuck off!'

Being me, I didn't think anything of it. But, about half an hour later, I'm standing where the barriers are and the guy's come towards me. He's pulled out a revolver on me and said, 'I'm gonna shoot ya!'

'You fucking what?'

I've *dived* over the fucking barrier, I swear to God, and grabbed the guy round his fucking neck. I've managed to take the gun off him and I've just started bashing him, bashing him, bashing him with it!

Clayton and all of the others came up and pushed me off of him. There was blood all over the fucking place. Someone called the police and they took him away.

London is a lot different from Birmingham – even though you've still got a gun culture in Birmingham, or someone can pull a baseball bat on you. London's got that name and there are loads of different firms, or posses, or gangs, whatever you want to call them. But at this time, in the nineties, when the guy pulled a gun I thought, *Fucking hell!*

I just carried on working as if nothing had happened, even though I had to go to the police station, and I was down there for about two hours. When I came back, the guys were waiting for me with the minibus. We spoke about it on the way back up; we had a laugh and a joke about it. I came back to work the following week and I just carried on doing what I was doing. Everyone was with me. I knew who I was working with; I knew these guys would stand by you.

I had about four or five guys come up to me and say, 'We're willing to give you some money if you don't turn up in court.'

I'm against the police – I don't do anything for the fucking Old Bill. But I thought at the time, *Fuck me, you're willing to take my life for something stupid! You wanted to shoot me over a little joke.*

People always say to me, 'What would you do if someone pulled a gun on you?' And my answer is: 'I don't know what I'd do. I don't know if I'd stand there and shit myself, piss myself or just start fucking crying: "Please don't kill me!"' But the main thing there was to jump for my life.

It was like an incident in Coventry with one of these P1 lads (a Midlands street gang): the guy was in his car at about three o'clock in the morning; I'm standing over here, he's over there and he's pulled a gun on me. I've just run across the fucking road, pulled my nunchukas out of my pocket and smashed the windscreen. He drove off. There were loads of people in the queue, but nobody really knew what was going on. He was at the front, behind a barrier, so I don't think a lot of people saw it – all they saw was me jump in and start bashing him.

Some of the guys on the door were wearing bulletproof vests even before then. I've worked in loads of places where the doormen have them on. I haven't worn one once, because if they're going to shoot you then they're going to fucking shoot you. A fucking arsehole's going to shoot you in the head if you wear a bulletproof vest. Someone in their right mind isn't going to shoot you anyway.

A lot of the doormen *do* wear bulletproof vests when they're going out of town to work, especially in London. I know that guys who work in Birmingham won't wear them, but they'll go to places like Manchester to work and they'll put them on. Whereas me, I just go as I am. The other doormen would say to me, 'Why aren't you wearing a bulletproof vest?' But I thought, *I can't afford one!*

I wear big baggy trousers just so I can kick, so I feel loose. I feel tight wearing normal clothes, but with a bulletproof vest you can't really move around and you sweat like fuck as well.

The rave scene brought the drug scene. The drug scene brought the guns in. The rave scene brought a lot of firms together too – a lot of firms that were fighting each other before became a lot closer. With the rave scene came Es – then came some other drugs. It all brought the criminal underworld together: gangs that were fighting started joining up, becoming friends, making bigger gangs and fighting other gangs.

But when that guy pulled a gun on me in London it shook me – it put a bit of fear into me because, despite my reaction at the time, I still don't know what I'd do in a similar situation. I think the doors at the time were a lot easier than they are now. There was a lot less trouble on the rave scene than there is now. The doors are a lot harder.

CHAPTER NINE

One of the best countries I've visited, fighting-wise, has got to be Hawaii. It was unreal: back in '94, I got to the airport and they gave me one of those 'Aloha' flower welcomes, then I was taken away in a stretch limo to my hotel. I got up in the early hours of the morning because I had to do *Good Morning Breakfast Hawaii*, and then there were radio interviews, press interviews and press conferences. When I was walking down Waikiki Beach under those big billboards, all I could see was my picture in lights: 'Dennis Alexio versus Barrington Patterson for the IKF World Heavyweight Championship'.

DEV

All down the years of training, we'd have a compulsory medical when he had a fight and nobody ever picked up on his eye. Nobody. And then we went to America. The medical is to check the fighter is in a fit state to compete – you've got to check the blood pressure especially and check them for any cuts and bruises, that type of thing. Check the eyes; check general fitness. Every fighter has to have a medical within a couple of hours or half a day before they fight. So you go for the fight and do the weigh-in, then you see the doctor and you get the rules, and then you fight, and that's the process – weigh-in, doctor and then go on. So, if they don't make the weight, they're not going to fight anyway. The doctors would always put the torch in his eyes and say, 'Look left, up and down,' just to check maybe for drugs, etc. We went over to Hawaii when he was fighting over there and the doctor said to him, 'Can you see?' and he said, 'Yeah!' The doctor made him put something over his eye and said, 'What am I doing?' He said, 'It's a little bit fuzzy but I can see the light.' I think the doctor said something like 'Remarkable' to him.

Throughout my whole kickboxing career, I never told anyone about my eye – never! I just didn't want people knowing. Dev didn't even know himself until I told him years down the line. If I had told them in the beginning I probably wouldn't have got as far as I have. Even though I had medicals, I always blagged them. I'd say I had blurred vision at that moment and I'd be OK in a bit. I'd always pass the fucking medical because they'd only ever check the one eye!

After I got better at kickboxing, the only person I told was Dev. Nobody else knew I was blind in one eye in any fight I had. But I never wanted him to stop any of my fights; I'd rather fight till I'm dead and I told him to never throw in the towel.

It was after the fight in Hawaii that I told him. I'm the joker of the gym so I was always having a laugh with him. But this time I was serious. 'Dev, I wanna tell you something.'

'What, Barrington?'

'I'm blind in one eye.'

He was shocked because there are guys with two eyes who haven't done what I've done. 'How come you never told me before?'

I didn't know whether to laugh or cry myself, but he never mentioned it after that. Everything was normal.

* * *

I was in no doubt that this was a big fight. This guy Dennis Alexio – who played Jean-Claude Van Damme's brother in a wheelchair in the movie *Kickboxer* – was originally from Los Angeles; the atmosphere was electrifying, with maybe 15,000 people crammed into the fight arena, and the promoter paid for everything: your full expenses, a little spending money plus your fight fee.

DEV

I know a few British guys have gone over there and just got knocked out in the first few rounds by Alexio – so I had calls from people to say, 'Be careful with the "Terminator".' 'Well we're always careful in all fights!' 'Especially this one.' Now, leading up to Alexio, they contacted me, they wanted a video of Barrington to sell for promotional reasons over there. In my head, I'm thinking, Yeah, I know what they're up to. *So I sent them the worst video of Barrington I could find. Afterwards, they sent it back and said, 'The quality wasn't good enough; can you send us something of Barrington training?' So I said to Barrington, 'I know what they're doing, they just want to study you.' So I made sure he did everything differently – different stance than he would normally fight in, different type of punches, different combination, and we trained in that way and then we sent them that video. So we knew – obviously they were training but when Barrington would jump in the ring it would be a different person altogether!*

On the way I stopped off in Los Angeles and then met Barrington and the others in Hawaii two days later. When I got there, they told me about the limousine waiting for them at the airport; they were going to press conferences each day and so forth. As usual, Barrington had already got fans following him around.

Our hosts were great. If they said they were to pick you up at 11 o'clock, they'd be there at 10 to 11. Come the day of the fight, they were supposed to be there to pick us up at two o'clock; they turned up at three. The night before the fight, I asked the promoter, 'Can I see the gloves?' I like to see the sort of gloves our fighter is going to wear because you can't wear your own; you have to bandage the hands as well.

As I said, we were late. We got to the fight and it seemed they did everything to make us feel uncomfortable. We got to the changing room, we had no air con. They did. I put his bandages on – they sent us gloves that were like the second standard, not first-class gloves. The stitching was further down so it meant that his hands couldn't go in: the stitching normally comes around the thumb but they were substandard gloves, so he couldn't get his hand in. So they announced to the crowd that we had arrived late and were not ready; eventually, they gave us some gloves that had been used by somebody else and they were wet. We obviously had to take his bandage off and do it up again. So as we walked out the crowd all started booing, and then eventually Dennis Alexio came in – a guy with about a dozen world title belts and all of them were shown around the ring.

Barrington was doing a lot better than they had expected. At the end of the first round, Barrington comes back and I'm there sorting his gum shield out and talking to him. You've got the red corner/blue corner and you've also got the two neutral corners. This ring girl literally *pushed me out of the way and I said, 'Why don't you go to the neutral corner?' And she said, 'My boss said I must come here.' She had to move me out of the way; we've only got a minute now so she's pushed me out of the way to go round the ring. I think Alexio was confused because Barrington was a different person to what he expected. Obviously, he couldn't do what he wanted in the fight and Barrington was clearly winning. Then, in the third round, he jump-kicked Barrington straight in the groin.*

About the third round, I was just jabbing away, jabbing away and coming forward. And, all of a sudden, he did a spinning back-kick that went *straight* in my groin! I just dropped straight away on the floor; it was the worst pain I've ever felt. I was on the floor, I was reeling around, I couldn't breathe properly, the pain was probably going to make me crap my box. Dev was over on the floor talking to me, and then someone came into the ring and said, 'If you don't get up and carry on fighting, you ain't gonna get paid.'

DEV

The heel is the most dangerous weapon you've got in martial arts. It's like using a battering ram, because the action of the heel is directly in and that's how he hit him in the groin. So obviously it got to the point where I thought, Impossible. *You could see the pain he was in and I thought,* You can't carry on. *The doctor came in and then somebody else came in and said, 'You've got to fight.' We said, 'No, it's impossible, he can't fight, he can't even stand up.' They said, 'You've got to fight; if you don't fight you don't get your expenses.' That means the flight – we paid for it but they were supposed to reimburse us. They wouldn't pay the flight, they wouldn't pay the expenses. In some countries, they make it quite strict, but with amateurs it's negotiable with expenses – so you can't actually get paid as such. If you are popular, your status and the fact that you can attract a crowd will make them pay you.*

Now normally there's a given time – different associations have their time, so let's say after four minutes a decision has to be made. Barrington was down for at least 15 minutes. If somebody's injured for that length of time, you can't continue; you need the hospital or some other serious medical attention. You should have a winner, a disqualification or a no-contest. But they made him fight on! Barrington was like a punch bag – Dennis Alexio had him in the corner and he was dipping his body shots around the kidney area. Alexio's a good boxer, he's a very good fighter – I think out of 70-something fights he's only ever lost one. It was painful watching from the corner, he was ramming those punches.

It was painful. I couldn't breathe, I couldn't kick – I couldn't do anything really. By the end of five rounds, the referee just stopped the fight.

But I was in Hawaii for a few days. I saw many Japanese tourists and plenty of shops – which is a weakness for me, as I love to shop. (Japan is one country where I wish I'd had the chance to fight; I feel I would have made my mark there.) At the time, I was ranked number two in world kickboxing and had already been a top five world-ranked fighter for a period. I lost to Alexio after five rounds in Hawaii, but it was the experience of a lifetime for me.

* * *

I entered the 1995 British Kickboxing Championships in Nottingham, where all of the best fighters in England turned up and fought each other. You've got about seven or eight weight categories and I got to fight at heavyweight. The W.A.K.O. (World Association of Kickboxing Organizations) Championships are a series of competitions that run every year. There were about eight of us from Dev's, a mixture of kickboxers and continuous fighters. You had to pay for your subscription and also your petrol to Nottingham. We all wanted to win in our weight divisions, including Gary Turner at light heavyweight.

There was a white lad from London who I was fighting for the first time. It wasn't much of a fight as it only lasted one round. I kicked him through the ropes and he didn't want to know after that; his corner threw the towel in.

You've then got to wind yourself down and go back to the changing room, but you've got to fight again in two or three hours, depending on how many people are in your category. I had to fight this other white lad only about an hour later, in three two-minute rounds. He was shitting himself when he saw me. The ref stopped the fight in the second round and I won with a technical knockout.

In the third fight, I was up against a good up-and-coming young lad. He was lighter than me and I had to use some dirty tricks against this fucker. I was holding him even when the referee was shouting, 'Stop, *stop!*' But he was throwing some punches and kicks and I was thinking, *Where the fuck are they coming from?* The guy was fast. I think he was from Newcastle, but I managed to beat him on points and I was crowned W.A.K.O. British Champion – for the fifth year in a row.

Whoever wins in their weight division gets to fight for England in the World and European Championships. In 1995, the World Championships were in the Ukraine, where I got to fight for the heavyweight title in full-contact kickboxing. A couple of weeks before, I had to go around and get the things I needed ready. There was a place in London where we had to have team photos taken in shirt and tie. The Sports Council didn't pay for any of our stuff; we even had to raise money for our fares to the fucking Ukraine! Altogether, there were about 30 fighters from England and the semi-contact karate lads were there as well.

The Ukraine was cold. (Even colder than Russia would be later!) We were in Kiev, next to the football stadium, where we met up with this little 10-year-old boy. He could speak English and so he became our interpreter. In the evening, he'd go home, give his mum some money, then come back and stay at our hotel with us. Everywhere we went he'd come with us.

I had two fights on the first day. The first was against a guy from Belarus, which I won, and then I fought a guy from Russia. He was a good fighter, but everyone I fought was a champion in their own country. I beat the Russian guy as well. There were about 15 guys in my category, but after the second fight you had to go and sit down for the rest of the day. You couldn't really leave as you were part of a team and had to cheer them on. You got there about 9am and it went on till 6 or 7pm.

The next day, I had a really hard fight. The guy just hit me and hit me and hit me. He kept hitting me with body shots but he couldn't put me down. My body has always been toned so it didn't really affect me. I think I just about edged that fight.

The third fight arrived and I thought, *I'm ready now!* I was suffering a bit with bruising but it didn't matter. I had to get on with my next fight. I fought this guy from Lebanon and beat him easily. I'd had three fights that day and they said to me, 'You've got through to the final, you're gonna fight at the final tomorrow.' I just said, 'No problem.' I took my gloves and pads off, found my mates in the crowd and cracked a few jokes with them. Then I said, 'Listen, I'm tired, I'm gonna get me some sleep.'

I was sleeping on the top tier of the bunks. I'd been asleep for about an hour when, all of a sudden: 'Wake up, wake up!'

'What?'

'Get up, get up, you have to fight now!' this guy said.

'They told me I'm fighting tomorrow.'

'No, you have to fight right now or you will be disqualified!'

'How the fuck am I supposed to fight now?'

Dev came over and I told him what they'd said. He went to see the organiser and they said the guy was right. I had about 10 minutes to warm up, get bandaged up and put my gloves on. I got my kit on and they told me I was fighting some guy called Wladimir Klitschko. I'd never heard of him, but we know him today as one of the World Heavyweight boxing champion brothers.

As I got into the ring, I said to Dev, 'Look at the fucking size of him!' He was up *there* and I was down *here*. Fucking hell! I was just under six feet tall and weighed about 16 and a half stone. He looked a full foot taller than me.

I came out in the first round and wanted to fight, but my body wouldn't do what I wanted it to. He was jabbing me and my head was flipping back. His front kicks went *boom! – boom!* – connecting every time and I couldn't move out of the way. I was cowering against the ropes and he was bashing me. The guy was so tall I just couldn't get out of the way. He was just tall and awkward. I couldn't get in there; I couldn't get a punch or kick in on him, to tell the truth. At the end of the first round, I went back to the corner and said, 'Dev, I'm fucked!'

'Shut up, man! Just get back out there and get on with the fight – shut up!'

I came out for the second round and the guy was trying to take my head off with some jabs. There were some big fucking kicks too! The second round ended and he won that. Then he won the third round and took the fight.

He won because I didn't get a chance to prepare properly. They'd told me I was fighting the next day. But he didn't knock me out. He won the gold medal and I took the silver, and I was happy with that. There were plenty of guys who came away with nothing. I was well chuffed with the silver; it put me up the world ratings ladder again. But, even on the plane, everyone was saying that they fucked me up and that I should have had the extra day's rest. We tried for years to get a rematch with Klitschko but he just didn't want to know. At least Dev said it was a job well done.

* * *

With me looking the way I do, bodybuilding has helped me with my kickboxing as well. Say you've got a fight; your opponent's never seen you, he's never heard of you, but, as soon as you come out in the ring and take your top off, he's going, '*Fuckin' hell*, look at this guy! Look at the size of him!' You've beaten him mentally already. You've just got to go in there and do the physical stuff. I fought a guy in Northampton called Dave Sharpe and he was a big, muscular guy as well. He was some black belt in taekwondo but he couldn't lift his fucking feet up. I went over to him and he was cowering down in the corner.

DEV

We went to a dinner show where he was fighting, in Northampton. He did his normal showboat stuff and he knocked this guy down and out, and he was just having a laugh – because Barrington is very, very respectful, there's no question about that. Somebody at the ring, sitting at one of the tables of this dinner show, was shouting at him and calling him a wanker. After they announced the winner, Barrington stormed off to the changing room and said, 'Right, I'm gonna get them,' and he started taking his bandages off. I said, 'Barrington, you can't do it – you're not doing it.' And he says, 'No, I am. I've never been disrespectful to you, I've always done what you've said – but I'm sorry, I can't listen to you today.' I thought, Shit, he means it! So I had to go find the door staff and say, 'Listen, I don't know if you saw what happened in the ring but Barrington's coming out – I can't even stop him and if I can't stop him then you guys won't.' So then they've obviously got these couple of guys who shouted at him and escorted them out of the place.

You'll probably notice that most of these fights were abroad, on the international circuit. I have always managed him and decided who he'd fight, or how and when the fight would be, what the rules were, etc. This is because of the type of fighter that Barrington was; he was an entertainer and the British public just can't cope with that, they don't like it. Because Barrington showboats, people will pay extra money to get him over to their country to fight because they like how he does things – he has a laugh. But in this country they seem to take it as showing off. Even the kickboxing public who were watching didn't like it. At one point, I just said, 'That's it,' and he didn't fight over here for a long, long time, we just went abroad.

He fought in the 1996 European Championships and made it to the final. I think there were 29 countries at the time; like the Olympics, it's a tournament and at the end you're a champion. But you're not a real 'pro', so he could fight as a pro amateur but still be in the amateur bouts. Barrington made it through to the final – he fought really well – but this Russian kid Almaz Gismeev was fast, hit him and run, switched. Barrington clearly lost the fight. But, after they announced it and Gismeev got his big cup, as they came out of the ring, all the kids ran to Barrington to get his autograph. He was surrounded! And this poor guy who had just become European

Champion Heavyweight was standing there with his trophy on his own.

When we went to Brazil in 1997 for the W.A.K.O. Pro Intercontinental, he had just as many supporting him. Barrington's like the Pied Piper! It was live on TV, the same channel that films Brazilian football. We should have gone there four months before but they were filming the football so they couldn't do it, they had to call the tournament off. It was their Independence Day so they allowed everyone to go to the sports centre for free; as you can imagine, it was absolutely rammed out with thousands of people. There was an area where they had demonstrations of capoeira, traditional karate and a great variety of martial arts – so it was like a big family day out and at night we had the kickboxing.

Apparently, you always get two sides – you got the side that supported Paulo Zorello and the side that supported another fighter. So they were supporting Barrington automatically, he had a lot of support over there. Kickboxing is big in Brazil. The same people watch both traditional martial arts events and kickboxing, so there were thousands there. That was his sweetest knockout.

My best result for England was in Brazil in 1997, which was the cream of the crop for me. The guy I fought was called Paulo Zorello, who had been in the Ukraine and told the W.A.K.O. that he wanted to fight me on Brazil's National Independence Day. They gave me a couple of videos to watch: this guy had never lost a fight and he was a top boxer. But he didn't want to fight Klitschko, he wanted to fight me. I'd got the fight, but when I was watching videos of him I thought, *How the fuck can I get near him?*

I fought in Sao Paulo at the Morumbi stadium. It was Brazilian National Independence Day, so they let everyone into the stadium free. I looked around and thought, *Imagine this place when there's a football match, it'd be jam-packed.* I went to the changing room and chilled out, and then walked outside with Andre, who's also a boxing trainer. I don't like sitting down any time before a fight. Some other fighters like to go to the changing rooms, put their bags down and go to sleep; I like to have a walk outside the stadium and get a feel for the crowd, to mingle and talk with friends. When I looked around this crowd, I realised that all these people were here to see me. Now I knew what it was like for all the boxers who fight in different countries. Everyone was there for the main attraction – it was fucking *me*!

My fight was just after the break; there had been eight or nine before mine. When the break came I thought, *It's time to get serious now*, so I went to the changing rooms to do a bit of stretching. I stripped off and warmed up, then put on my jockstrap and bandages. I wore white trousers that had a Jamaican flag on one side and an English flag on the other, specially made by a designer called Paula Christie.

I didn't really train that hard for the fight; I really liked the fights but I was just a lazy trainer. I don't think anyone gave me much of a chance of beating this guy. Zorello was a boxer and a kickboxer. I don't think he'd lost many fights so I didn't think I was going to beat him; he was actually the Heavyweight Champion of the World at the time. So when Dev said to me this would be a chance to fight for the World Heavyweight title, I said, 'I might as well go for it.' Like I said, I slacked off, I didn't really do a lot of training, I thought, *A fight's a fight, just go and fight.* Not only did I not give myself a chance of beating him but no one else did either.

I got on the bags. I had no footwear for the fight – you can put bandaging on your feet, but that's it. I wore brand-new six-ounce fingerless gloves, thinking to myself, *This is* the *fucking fight, man. It's all about me now, this is my fucking time!*

About 20 minutes later, a guy came in the changing room and said, 'We're ready for you now.' They called me 'Pit Bull' – as in English pit bull terrier. I had my music on – I am a champion, so I walk out to 'Walk like a Champion'. I was ready now. I wanted to start playing to the crowd.

I came out for the first round and the guy was like, *BAM! BAM!* Where were these kicks and punches coming from? I don't think I even probably threw one or two good punches or kicks in the first or second round. I was just stalking him. I stood there with my hands out, just carried on.

Bang! The guy has hit me and I've gone, *Is that it?* to the crowd. But he was punching and kicking the head off me, as he was particularly fast and I was carrying two to three stone more weight. He did a little shuffle and came at me.

I came out for the third round and I was tired – fucking tired! He got me in the corner of the ring, I backed off and he was beating the shit out of me. Then I just went *bang!* 'Ya fucker!' He flew back in the ring. I rushed at him and got him down on the floor. I grabbed him and started banging him. The referee said, 'Get up and fight.' We stood up and I kicked him. I gave him a roundhouse kick, then a left and a right punch, and the guy was out. I didn't just win the fight, I did it in style – I really took the piss out of him before I knocked him out in the third round. I think I threw a jab and my right hand came straight over the top and caught him. I think it was either his neck or his temple. The Brazilian did get up but immediately toppled over again. The guy just fell on the floor. I was motioned to my corner and I recall thinking, *Please don't get up – I've had enough. I can't fucking do any more!* He crawled to the rope, got up and just fell back down. And I thought, *Fuck me, I've won!* Alexio was history – I'd knocked Paulo Zorello out, knocked him *clean out*, in the third round. The intention was there: if it caught him it caught him, if it didn't it didn't

– but I got lucky. Nice one. It was a 12-round fight, but it only went to the third.

Everyone started jumping up and down, the crowd was going fucking wild! Dev and Andre jumped through the ropes and were hugging me. The announcer said, 'The winner is Pit Bull Patterson, all the way from England!'

My promoter had wanted me to put on a good fight. He'd seen me fight a couple of times in my kickboxing career and knew I was a crowd pleaser. You could be the best fighter in the world but still be really boring. The crowd pay to see something worthwhile, so let them get their money's worth.

I got paid about 6,000–7,000 Euros after the fight, cash and carry. I'd taken one or two kicks to my leg so I put some ice on it. We stayed and watched the rest of the fights, then we all went out and got fucking pissed. I wasn't a drinker in those days, but I was knocking back the brandies.

I had to do radio and TV interviews and press conferences. People didn't leave me alone before or after the fight. They were walking up to me because they'd seen me live on Dutch TV. As I walked around the stadium, people came up to me and said, 'You're a good fighter – we've come all the way from England and you've entertained us.'

DEV

Barrington has natural strength, because for such a big guy he's got flexibility, he's quite fast. Sometimes people over-train – Barrington trained probably not as hard as he should, but there was that natural thing, he's a natural athlete. The thing about Zorello is he was neat – very clean, very tidy. You look at the first round and the way he threw a combination – one-two-three punches then kick – he was really good, and when he hit Barrington with all of that one-two-three punches then kick, he had a fight on his hands.

You normally try sussing out the power the other fighter has got, and his stance. You might say, 'Keep moving to your left,' you might work out that his right hand is not very good, 'so if you go towards it you'll be OK with that, but don't go towards that left hook.' On this night, the thing was: 'Don't go backwards – stalk him, keep going forward,' which is what he did. His punches that he'd worked on, that he'd practised, just went over the top. The thing is about that fight, they obviously saw Barrington fight Klitschko: nobody knew anything about Klitschko then, they didn't realise what type of fighter Barrington had just fought – we didn't, nobody knew. So because Klitschko won they thought, Well, it'd be a great display on Independence Day in front of thousands, live on TV. There was no way on this planet that they expected Zorello could possibly lose. They didn't even bring the world title belt, because as far as they saw it he was this big black guy with loads of muscles who can't fight – and that's how they looked at him.

* * *

In the late 1990s, I had a fight against the champion that they labelled 'the Black Bear of Russia' in some magazine. When we got there, it was unbelievable! I thought that people wouldn't like a black man going to Russia, but they were all over me like a rash. It was cold and I went there wearing thermals and gloves. It was so fucking cold, but I remember people queuing up for ice cream!

I went to the top restaurants in Russia and the food was shit! So we found a currency shop where you could buy westernised food. Russian food is bear meat, potatoes and some horrible vegetables – that is, brown bear meat, *grizzly* bear meat.

The stadium in Moscow was chock-a-block. I had a walk around playing 'spot the black man'; me and Dev were the only black people there. I went to get changed and I was crapping myself. I had to tell myself: 'I'm 'ere now and I've established myself as a reasonable fighter. *I'm 'ere!*' But the guy I was fighting was no mug. He was the Russian champion and he'd never lost or been put down before.

I got changed and warmed up. Then I came out and made a fucking big entrance, man! I'd only been fighting a few years but I'd had up to 10 fights. I played my Buju Banton and wore one of those Russian hats. I had big sunglasses on and a red poncho. I was dancing to my music and the crowd loved it. Then I took all my stuff off and stood there.

DEV

This was an international. We took a team from GB to Moscow to fight against a team over there. That is obviously a big show, with a 10,000-capacity crowd. It was at the Olympic ice rink and, of course, it's quite a serious event. I was in the changing room to do the warm-up, getting ready to do his bandages, and we're waiting for the cue. Time to go now: so I've set him up, walked out and Barrington would normally follow behind me. So I'm walking down, I've continued walking and I've got towards the ring and I'm looking behind: 'Where the hell is Barrington?' I couldn't see him anywhere! Then, all of a sudden, I could hear the crowd laughing. Now Barrington had set it up with one of the other guys – because he knew I'd have said no if he'd told me what he was going to do – that he was going to walk down the catwalk, as they had a fashion show on that night, instead of walking where the fighters were supposed to go! Whereas we'd have a kickboxing show over here, they'd make it a night out. So they had a fashion show with models walking down; later they put a group on, later still they'd put the kickboxing on. So strutting down with these dark glasses on, the Russian hat and a big cape, everybody was howling at Barrington! And I'm by the ring – I had no idea they were doing it. Because he knew I would have said, 'No chance – walk this way!'

He comes out and I'm thinking, *I'm gonna have a fucking fight here on my hands, I gotta put on a good show now!* It was a big five-rounder and I was sweating a bit. The first round was probably about even. I kicked him a couple of times and thought, *Fuck me, this guy can take some hits!* He hit me a couple of times too, but I didn't think much of it.

The second round was still even. We were both jabbing and working nicely. Then the third round came and I went all out. I put a couple of combinations on him – *bang, bang, bang!* The guy went down and bounced back up again. The ref gave him a standing count.

Then I came out in the fourth round and I was getting really tired. He was catching me with some good kicks and I was thinking, *Where the fuck are these punches and kicks coming from?* The fifth round was really hard and I had to dig deep. I was tired and drawn. The crowd was behind him, chanting. When the bell rang for the end of the fifth, I dropped to my knees and thought, *Thank fuck for that!*

Then they said, 'The winner, from England . . .' and I thought, 'Yeah!' I wasn't tired anymore. Afterwards, I got changed and everyone wanted to have their photos taken with me – especially the Russians. People were crowding around me and bringing me presents like ice-hockey sticks and key rings. The Russian fighter came on the microphone to say thank you for the fight and that I was a strong guy.

I went to the after party and there was loads of vodka and cognac on the table. The party was on a boat and it was full of sexy women. Most of them were hos but I wasn't bothered about getting my end away. I was sat there with Dev having a good time, eating and drinking. I said to Dev, 'Superstar!' I was knocking back vodka, about six of them, before Dev said, 'We're going now.'

I got up and *boom!* Straight on my arse! Dev and a couple of the guys had to lift me on to their shoulders and carry me off the boat, back to my hotel room. We got into the hotel lift and apparently I collapsed.

I got up next morning and said, 'Dev, somebody put me into bed and put a bucket next to me.'

He explained that he'd done it, as I'd been caning the vodka and couldn't stand up and all this shit!

I went back to Russia about a year later for a wicked fight. I'd become established in kickboxing by then. The second one was in St Petersburg.

DEV

On the back of the St Petersburg Times, *which apparently is the most distributed newspaper in the world, there's a little story about Barrington: It says 'The Monster Of Kickboxing Comes To Our City' – I've actually got the clipping. When we were in Russia, Barrington couldn't walk down the road or go to the shops without people crowding him, asking for autographs and photographs; he was like a magnet that attracts people. And what he decided to do this time, halfway through the fight, was to give this fighter his face – but little did he know that this guy had a hundred-plus boxing fights. Barrington literally put his face out and said, 'Go on, hit it!' and the guy went, WHAM! Muhammad Ali used to ride the punch, but Barrington just took it. It was unbelievable. It took me the rest of the fight to try to revive him, because he was on another planet. I actually thought when he did that he was going to dodge it – but he didn't! To take a punch off a top boxer is a different thing. Of course he didn't win that fight – he just about survived!*

He'd had a lot of fights. I felt the shivers go straight down my legs and right up my body.

CHAPTER TEN

I got into cage fighting after I'd had a kickboxing fight in Holland at the end of the 1990s. A guy came to my dressing room and asked if I wanted to have a Mixed Martial Arts fight. I asked him what it was, and he told me it was 'where you fight on the ground'. So my trainer said yeah, I could give it a go. There was money in it, after all – nothing like today's appearance money, which has got better and better, but I only ever fought for money. I didn't know what a 'mixed fight' was though. I'd never heard of it.

You can call it cross-training: I'll fight in a completely different discipline to what I'm used to. I'm used to doing kickboxing: all of a sudden, I've got to do karate, shinko kai, I've got to fight K-1. It's a mix: different rules, different moves that you can't use in this one but you can use in that one.

My first heavyweight MMA fight was in October 1999, in Holland, against Sander MacKilljan, who'd won four fights and lost one. But before that I had a couple of kickboxing fights. I fought a black guy named Mo T – 'Big Mo T' they call him. He was huge with great big arms, and he was unbeaten.

DEV

MMA is a very important event in Holland. It's not just a bunch of lads going out for a beer and to watch a fight; people go out to see the shows with their families or their wives and girlfriends. Boxing is not very popular, football is their first game and the second is kickboxing/Mixed Martial Arts. It's been like that for a long time. How top boxers are looked on in this country is exactly the same as how these martial arts people – kickboxers and Mixed Martial Arts fighters – are in Holland. They are household names and can make a living from fighting.

We used to go to Holland quite a lot, always to Groningen, which is in the North of Holland. Barrington became a bit of a legend up there, so they almost adopted him as if he were one of theirs. When they had a show, we'd always go and fight up there, and he became a crowd pleaser. It was a plus that they appreciated what he was. It's only in the latter part of Barrington's career that they appreciated him over here. So the people from the south – they have this north–south divide too – all used to come up and watch Barrington because all the big shows were down in the Amsterdam area. They wanted Barrington to fight at one of the shows, but these guys from the north said, 'Barrington is ours, you can't have him.' They would say to me, 'Listen, these guys will try and contact you for him to fight, and we're asking you as a friend and as a sportsperson that you stay with us up north,' because they'd always buy the good fights and take them down south. Barrington fought again and they came up and watched how he crowd-plays, and they were now asking me. I said, 'Sorry.' Eventually, he fought against this shinko kai fighter, which is like low-kick/bare-fist/no punches to the face, a pure Japanese discipline. And then, after he knocked that big fellow out, we went out for a meal with the Dutch promoters. We had a little talk: they'd obviously made a backroom deal which I'd never known about for Barrington to fight down south. So he fought Sander MacKilljan.

Barrington started off by dancing when they introduced him; he'd come into the ring and start dancing around with the ring girl. They did that for a good load of fights wherever he fought in Holland; they imported this girl to come in the ring and dance with him.

I've come into the ring dancing to my usual music – 'Walk like a champion / Talk like a champion' – and these two girls are dancing beside me. But this Sander

MacKilljan guy came into the ring with these two ginormous bodybuilders – they made *me* look small, they were so huge.

DEV

There were times when his dance was on the catwalk – he'd walk in and dance all the way down. The girls would stop with him about halfway down, they'd come in the ring and dance. Sometimes the dances lasted longer than the bloody fights!

MacKilljan was a big fellow – really big. We didn't know the background to Mixed Martial Arts because I was purely a kickboxing coach. So we trained really hard for this because they were paying us good expenses. I didn't really understand about groundwork or anything like that. Barrington went out and started the round; dropped him. And normally you'd jump on somebody when you knocked them down. We didn't do any groundwork; we just trained Barrington to stand up. I know when he knocked MacKilljan down they expected Barrington to jump on him and start choking him and so on, but he just stood up, put his hands on his hips and the crowd went berserk!

I knocked him down on the floor and they weren't too happy – I was expected to jump on him. But it was like he's not only had a beating but I humiliated him, I took the piss out of him. He was hitting me and I was showboating. He'd be at my thighs and I'd be standing there brushing my legs. And I beat him – but it wasn't just that I beat him, I also took the piss out of him and the crowd loved it. Then I ended up knocking him out and, ever since that moment, I got offers to appear on fight bills. It wasn't just about being a fighter but being a crowd pleaser as well. I'd play up to my opponent and try to make him look silly; even if I lost a fight, the crowd always wanted entertainment.

DEV

The Mixed Martial Arts is a mixture where you can do a jiu-jitsu-type thing when you go on the floor; you fight on the ground; you can hold and kick; you can wrestle. But general kickboxing is stand-up and all kicks are above the waist. In Mixed Martial Arts, they use elbows and knees, so that's quite different. It's not the sort of thing that would be suitable for children. I suppose they do it now, but it's still a bit more brutal.

In this day and age, it *is* suitable for children, there's more of a framework. Because, when they started Mixed Martial Arts, it was like that Brazilian thing in the cage: vale tudo, where it's more brutal than MMA. Because with vale tudo you could head butt, you could kick 'em in the groin, you could stamp 'em on the floor. It's Brazilian street fighting, that's where it all originated from. But when it got to a few years down the line, they started coming out with other rules. Of course, when it started getting more popular, then the UFC (Ultimate Fighting Championship) thing started coming in, so it dropped some of the rules – it was a bit more brutal because you could head butt and things like that. But now it's got more popularised, the UFC's bought out all the other forms: MMA, free fighting. You have boxers coming onside and trying to get into MMA as well, and getting annihilated.

When I took the piss out of Sander MacKilljan and beat him, they put me with a Russian guy who was totally different. After that, when I beat the Russian guy, I was fighting one of MacKilljan's trainers; then I fought another guy who was a trainer of that guy, then another guy who was the trainer of that guy, and it just went on.

For a couple of years, I did both kickboxing and MMA at once. Of course, a lot of promoters over here knew that I could pull a crowd. There were a lot of them asking me to fight, but the money wasn't good so I preferred to go to Holland – the purse is much better in Holland plus it's a weekend away. Say the show you're fighting in is on a Sunday, the crowds are like 20- or 30-odd thousand people watching a fight. You're fighting over here for a couple of hundred people and the promoters want to pay you peanuts. You're there for a weekend, enjoying yourself, doing what you've got to do for a weekend, plus you're fighting in front of a big crowd of people.

After that, I had about six heavyweight MMA fights

one after the other. MMA is unbelievable in terms of what the training demands from you; it's a young man's sport. I don't think I could go through all that again for another fight. If I was weak on anything, it was the grappling work. I trained for it but I'm a fighter who would rather stand up and have it; I've always been 100 per cent confident when standing up, but probably only 50 per cent if gone to the ground. So I was always defensive against being taken down. The training is also a lot harder if you're a ground fighter and it can take a lot out of you.

DEV

They were offering us money and Barrington wanted to fight – if there wasn't money, there was still the opportunity to fight and a weekend away. So we went. But after we watched the other fights and we came back, then I realised there was a little bit more to it. So that's when we started going to the MMA fighter Matthew Evans – rather than trying to learn it, I just said, 'Right, we're better off going to somebody who knows that stuff.' So he would go to Mattie and learn the groundwork and we would do the stand-up stuff. So, when we would go back now to fight, I would take Mattie as a corner as well, rather than try to teach him something I don't really know about.

This is really going back, back, back – but at the very start Barrington used to fight in this ECKA (English

Contact Karate Association) championship. So he fought in every discipline, which not many people can do. He fought in light contact, semi-contact, K-1 (Japanese kickboxing), full contact, cage fighting, kyokushinkai and free fighting – all at a very good level.

After that, people just wanted to fight me and they all came from the same fucking gym! I fought one of my first opponents' friends and his trainer after that. They were all from the same camp and they all wanted a shot at me. I felt good in myself because I'd taken my first opponent out in style and felt like I'd accomplished something. I beat him nicely and the crowd loved it. I was trying something different for the first time and I'd won. It had been mainly a stand-up fight and neither of us wanted to go to the floor. But to go further in MMA I knew I had to learn a lot more. There would be times when you *had to* go to the floor.

I did judo for about four or five years, but this was a totally different thing. So I had to find somewhere that actually did the jiu-jitsu and all that and go and learn it, even though I didn't like doing it. I had to train for the way I was fighting, though I would do all my fights standing up if I could.

It did feel strange. If I was fighting and I'd got him on the ground, instead of jumping on him and trying to take him on the ground, I'd stand there and say, 'Get up, man.'

I continued with my kickboxing which helped with

MMA, because all fights start standing up – you go to the floor if you've got to go to the floor. People in England had started to hear about me. My name had started to come through and the promoters were asking me to fight – 'We'll give you £200–300.'

I thought, *Fuck you, man! Why should I fight for that much when I can get six to seven grand fighting in Holland?* That was the mistake I made in my career. I should have taken the smaller fights instead of relying on one fight a year. I should have taken those fights in England and used my experience when I went back to Holland. But I thought it was better to wait till the end of the year and earn six to seven grand.

I then was asked to fight a Russian guy called Stanislav Nuschik who was a sambo wrestler – it's a Russian style of wrestling and I knew he'd want to go to the floor. I was going to have to train even harder now, to do more groundwork. I trained for six weeks leading up to the fight. Everything was going brilliantly to plan. But this was a year after the first MMA fight, so it was a long time. It's up to us if we want to do a bit extra, but I don't research other fighters. I don't try to study their personalities; I just try to take them as they come. Every fighter is different.

The fight was in Holland. The hotel and food were lovely, and the reception I got at the airport was unbelievable. Even immigration asked me for my autograph. I thought, *Fuck me, I must be getting better!*

I'd made a name for myself in kickboxing and now I was doing the same in MMA. The reception was very different from the first fight now that I had a reputation.

Everywhere you go in Holland there are MMA posters. It's more established and you get crowds of 20,000, including families and even footballers coming to watch shows. Apart from football, it's all kickboxing and MMA over there. It's big time!

I had media interviews before the fight; I had to do a medical and a weigh-in too. Everything went to plan. It was the same as any other fight: get up in the morning; have some breakfast; go for a walk. Everything was still the same and I tried not to change anything. The girl I was seeing at the time came with me, which was nice. (I can't remember which girl – I got through so many!) Andre came again and so did my mate Mattie Evans – who's a Coventry bloke who's had a few fights and is a good teacher. He was one of the people trained by Geoff Thompson, who used to be a doorman and did that book *Watch My Back*.

Outside the stadium was chock-a-block. I walked around meeting people, signed a few autographs and had pictures taken with the crowd. I got back to the changing room and had a rest, then had another walk outside the stadium. I like to walk around and have a laugh with my trainers.

At one of my weigh-ins, it had kicked off before the fight. I've had a few altercations like that, but for this fight the weigh-in was normal. We'd had our photos taken and shook hands – 'See you on the date.'

Just before the fight, I got changed, put on my gloves and box and wore shorts this time. I did wear trousers for the first fight, but you should try to fight as light as possible really. When you go back to your corner, you are heavy with sweat and retained water.

Nuschik came out first. Then my music came on and I was dancing and jumping around. My mates in the background were shouting, 'ZULU! ZULU! ZULU!' I came out strutting my stuff, with two showgirls dancing by the side of me. I was just playing to the crowd and they were fucking loving it! Then the music stopped and it was time to get down to business.

The ref called us out to fight. We shook hands. As soon as the guy came out, he went straight for my legs. I thought, *Fucking hell, this guy's fast, man!* So I stayed centre of the ring and started kicking – kicking – kicking. As soon as he shot forward, I'd step back and hit him with a low kick. This went on till the end of the first round.

I went back to my corner and Dev said, 'You gotta stop him, you gotta stop him!' This is where my kickboxing came in – because I'd been kicking him in the legs, in the second round he just couldn't stand up. He was on the floor, so I jumped on him and started pounding him. I gave him about six or seven punches and the ref stopped the fight. I strutted my stuff around the ring, waving to the crowd, blowing kisses.

All I heard was 'Patterson Zulu! Patterson Zulu!' It was good to use my kickboxing experience, it still came in useful. I won that one nice and easy, but I knew there were bigger fish to fry.

At the after party, I didn't say much to the Russian, but we had a good time. Our girlfriends were there, we were drinking and I'd won two out of two. It was a little more money this time and the 20,000 crowd had been great.

On the Monday, I caught the plane back to Birmingham International. I had a big trophy in my hand and people kept asking where I'd got it – which was nice. I went home and just chilled out with the missus and the kids. It was lovely but I couldn't wait for my third fight.

A couple of months later, the promoter rang me and said, 'I've got a guy who says he wants to fight you.'

'Who is this fucking guy?'

'He's called Hans Nijman.' He was the trainer of the first MMA fighter I fought. The promoter said he'd been shouting his mouth off in Holland about fighting me. The first time he was looking for me, I was going through a lot of shit with my wife and got into loads of fucking trouble. I went through hell and it ended by me getting locked up in prison.

I was married to my second wife, Linda, at the time. After a while, I'd started working a bit in Spain, doing security for the rave scene over there and then coming back over here. I was working at rave clubs like

Manumission and Es Paradis in Ibiza. Guys there used to say to me, 'How the fuckin' hell you stay awake?'

I'd say, 'Listen, as long as I've got my black coffee and my girls around me, I'll be all right.' I was never into taking drugs to stay awake. When I saw guys on pills or sniff or whatever, I would just take a step back and really look at those people. I'd think to myself, *Fuckin' hell, man, all this big hard-man rep!* They were not big hard-men any more because they were off their faces on the pills: 'All right mate, how yer doing? Kiss kiss!' And that's when a lot of faces that would have been rivals now became friendly with one another.

When I was in back in Coventry, I saw the acid-house scene get massive. Everyone was getting together under one roof and just kissing each other, shaking or joining hands and loving each other. All the lads were at it: Coventry Legion guys, Villa. Amnesia was a big club on the rave scene at the time, but one of the guys there committed suicide.

I may not have been into the raves, but I was messing around a bit in my private life. When you're messing around though, you don't expect your wife to be messing around too!

So I ended up finding her out. I found the boyfriend, kicked her mum's door in, went in there, hammered him – as you do, right? I was on bail conditions to keep away from the house after that. Everything leads off from there: it was a messy divorce; I had an injunction to keep away from her, so every time I rang there or went round the house to pick up my things she'd call the police and say, 'He came round the house, he's sitting outside in his car, he's driving next to me in the road, he's chasing me in his car.' I'm getting pulled every week for silly little things: me and my mate got dragged on to the floor by armed police because I was supposed to be driving round with a bloody gun in my car – and all they caught me with was a machete. When I went to court, they had to give me my machete back.

MAL

His ex went off with another bloke; he was at home and Barrington phoned the house. He goes to Barrington, 'Who the fuck do you think you are?' Barrington says, 'I'll show you who the fuck I am!' He goes down there, kicks down the front door and then kicks this guy in the face, knocks him out. The police get called: 27 red dots on his body, that's how they dealt with Barrington.

There was this other guy and he had a bit of beef with Barrington; he bottled him on his head. Whenever he saw him, Barrington would beat the shit out of him; he'd just say to remind him whenever we saw him.

So I ended up splitting up from her; I had numerous other girls on the side and ended up seeing one called Lucy. But all of a sudden I pissed Linda off one day and she told the police. I ended up getting locked up for five or six weeks in Winson Green. Dev came up and said what he had to say in court.

DEV

He was in a cell on remand and he was supposed to be going away in three weeks to fight. Because he had this big fight, I knew he was good and ready and there was potential for him to become a regular fighter and make a good living. So I took the fight contract over, spoke to his solicitor and showed them what getting locked up was going to do to him. I wasn't 100 per cent sure that I got through, because they might have said, 'Oh well, his loss – he knew he had these things coming up, why did he jeopardise it?' But the judge didn't want to take that chance away from him, which was fantastic. That was one thing that I understand stopped him from going to prison. It was coming up; he was going to fight Hans Nijman and we had the contract. I was on the phone to the promoters saying, 'He might be, he might not be,' and in the end he got out. Thanks to the justice system!

A couple of times, when he's had a row in town and he's going to sort someone out, just through respect I've been able to say, 'Hey, come on, Barrington – leave it! It's not worth it! What are you going to gain except a prison sentence?' He actually listens. Barrington has got a heart of gold and I have seen him in tears. But he has a reputation and I suppose few people have seen that side of him. *The way that people talk about him makes it seem worse.*

Deep down, he is a gentle giant, but on the other side he is like a lion that is almost tamed. I trust him; he is reliable. When he has lost a fight, he takes it well, with no excuses. He has respected, supported and stayed loyal to ECKA, our karate and kickboxing organisation. The kids at the dojo think the world of him.

If it wasn't for having my friends and trainers around me, I'd probably be the same person now as I was back then. Dev turned up in court and said a lot for me, telling the court I had an important fight coming up. Prison was all right though – I was sound, as soon as I got in there I knew a lot of people and a lot of people knew me. The only thing was that I couldn't train. You can punch the bags but you can't kick them.

All I could think about was my wife and my kids. It really fucked my head up, but I'd broken my bail conditions for about four or five different charges and was on remand for six weeks. The food was shit too. Usually, when I train, I get up early and have a bowl of porridge with a couple of bananas. After I've trained, I'll have a couple of boiled eggs with some toast and a cup of coffee. But after 7pm I won't eat any carbs, just protein. I might have some fish or eggs, maybe an apple too, but I don't eat that much at that time of night.

In prison, I just kept thinking, *I want this fight, I want this fight, I wanna get out!* On the day of my trial, my trainer Dev turned up at court with all these fucking papers. He told the judge, 'Barrington's got a really important fight on this date,' and showed the poster. When I got a conditional discharge I thought, *Fucking nice one, Dev!* I'd really thought I was going to get sent down. But I got out – and knocked Nijman the fuck out!

* * *

So I was up against one of the top fighters in Holland at the time. I'd just split up with my wife and all I could think about in prison was having this fight and getting out to see my kids. I came out on the Wednesday and had to go to Holland on the Friday to fight on the Sunday. There wasn't much training I could do in two days and, even if I did, it wouldn't make much of a difference. I knew deep down in my heart I could go out there and win – even without the training. I was in the mood anyway. I'm a fighter and my heart was already there.

Nijman was one of the first MMA fighters in Holland and this guy was deadly. Dev showed me a video of him and he had a lethal kick on him. On Friday, we flew from Birmingham International and the promoter met us at Amsterdam airport. I just chilled out and went out at night, had a little perv around Amsterdam – as you do. I got back in nice and early as Dev was on my case: 'You gotta be back in by 12 o'clock.' I got in about two.

The next day, I had to do the regular TV interviews, the medical, meet the other fighter and have pictures taken. Then I was free to do what I wanted. I just chilled out and played cards with my friends.

On Sunday, the weigh-in was all right. We shook hands. Everything was fine and there were about 300 people there. To tell the truth, I don't think anyone gave me much of a chance for this fight. Dev said, 'If he catches you with that kick, you're gonna get knocked out.' He was the favourite.

I came out first, turned and looked at him. I thought, *Fuck you, you're going down, ya cunt!* He'd been giving it all that, speaking on Dutch TV: 'Barrington thinks he can come over here and take the piss out of other fighters.' I think he thought I was trying to disrespect them by talking when I was fighting, but this was good press and the promoters could blow it up a bit.

The fucking crowd were unbelievable! I've never seen anything like it. Twenty-odd thousand were there and there was a small section from Groningen all cheering for me. I think the whole of Amsterdam was cheering for him.

DEV

There were a few locals cheering for him as well, because Nijman was working on the doors and he's one of these characters who wasn't that well liked. There were people who were for Barrington totally, even though he was the guest or the foreigner. They were saying that Barrington was the first foreigner they'd taken to; the Dutch fighter usually always gets the crowd more than anybody else, but in the fights they always cheered more for him.

In the first round, I sent him to the floor with a body throw. I got on him and started punching, but he managed to get me off. We were on the floor and the referee told us, 'Stand up.' I took my eyes off him for one second and felt a breeze go past my face. His kick had just missed my head. If it had been two inches closer, he would have taken it off.

In the second round, I thought, *Fuck this, I can't last the fight.* I came out and caught him with a right uppercut. I wanted to fight on but I knew I wasn't fit enough. I just wanted to get it over and done with. I think I caught him with a left hook and sent the guy breakdancing. Usually, I'd jump on him and start pounding him, but I just stood there and watched him try to get up. He tried to pull himself up on the ropes but fell down. I thought, *You fucking cunt! What have you got to say for yourself now?* I took my gum shield out and started playing to the crowd: 'Who's number one now? I just took your number one!'

Before the fight most of the crowd had been cheering for him. When the ref put my hand up, I walked around the ring shouting, 'I'm number one! I'm number one!' The feeling was unbelievable, especially as I didn't train for the fight and I wasn't fit. I'd caught him with a combination and, with a little luck, put him to sleep.

When I'd hit him with that combination, I'd thought, *Please don't get up. Please* do not *fucking get up!* I knew that I was lucky and not fit enough to last two or three rounds. When I fight, I block out the crowd; all I can hear are my coaches and trainers, but it was time to get back to the drawing board.

The referee put my hand in the air and said, 'The winner, Barrington "Zulu" Patterson!' I thought, *Yeah, that's fucking me!* and all this tinsel came falling from the sky. It took me 15 minutes to get to my changing room because I got mobbed when I came out of the ring. I was signing autographs and having pictures taken.

When I got back to the changing room, Dev had a right go at me, because I could have got knocked out. We all had a laugh about it. I had a shower and then we all sat down to talk about the fight: if I'd have trained, how different would it have been? But at the end of the day I won, and that's the most important thing.

With hand on heart, I can say that was the only fight that I didn't do any training for. I went out there, did my best and beat a legend. I knew there would be more fights to come and more money, because I was winning. I'm a good fighter and a crowd pleaser, so they would want me to come back. I play up to the crowd and put bums on seats, I give them their money's worth. How many English guys have been to Holland and done what I did? I came, I saw, I conquered.

CHAPTER ELEVEN

In 2002, new promoters came in and I got offers from Cage Rage, but I wasn't going to fight for just two or three grand. I told Dev I wouldn't get out of bed for that. I was used to getting 6,000–7,000 Euros so why should I bother, considering the crowds I got in Holland? Dev was ringing me every day, saying the promoters were offering me a fight here and a fight there. 'How much, Dev?' It could be a few hundred or a couple of grand. 'I ain't fighting for that shit!'

As I said earlier, I should have taken those fights. A couple of months later, the promoters rang me and asked if I wanted to fight a guy called Joop Kasteel.

'Yeah I'll fight him. Send me the DVDs of his fights.' They sent me three DVDs and I thought, *Look at the size of that bastard!* I did a bit of homework on him and it turned out he'd been a bodybuilder. People look at me and think I'm big, but this guy was huge! He's got the height to go with it, whereas I'm only five foot eleven. He's six foot plus and massive. I watched the DVDs and thought, *He's still human, I'm gonna try and take this fucker.* I trained really hard for this fight. The promoter told me to go to Holland if I wanted proper training, so I would go over on Friday and come back on Sundays most weekends. They put me up in hotels and I trained, trained, trained!

DEV

Joop Kasteel was a monster. Somebody's got the photo: Barrington and the guys, one of them's Mattie, and Kasteel is standing behind us. He dwarfs all of us, even Barrington. That's how big he is, he's huge. I'm not sure if Kasteel's his real name, because 'Kasteel' means 'castle' and he is like a castle.

He's not as tall as the Klitschkos, he's only about six three, six four, but he's massive.

I had three wins from three fights; I can't remember his record but I think it was touching double figures at the time. He was a big bastard but I heard his stamina was shit. So I upped my training, my food and my running. I upped everything. I'm a big, muscular guy, so I was mainly working on my fitness. Most of my sparring was done in Holland but my fitness training was at Dev's gym.

I went to Holland because there weren't many guys that I could spar with. It was the best training I've ever had. The promoters paid for everything and I didn't spend a penny. I had six weeks of hard training and it was a buzz being out in Amsterdam with about 30 of my mates. Andre and Dev were there. Andre has been at most of my fights and he pushes me hard. He'll say, 'Come on, Baz, come on, Baz, you gotta do it!' He encourages me to go further.

This fight got a big build-up because we were two big lumps. He's about half a stone heavier than me and, when we stood together at the weigh-in, he said something that I didn't like. I went for him and he went for me. The coaches and trainers had to jump in and separate us. The TV cameras were there so it made for even more hype. That was on live Saturday-morning TV, so all the people who had seen this scuffle turned up for the show.

When I got to the stadium, oh my gosh, man! There were 20-odd thousand people but there were still queues and the last tickets were running out. On Sundays, you got everyone from families to top footballers and Dutch singers there. It was a big place and the layout was unbelievable.

I was walking around the stadium, mingling with people and doing my same old routine. Dutch people were coming up to me, wishing me luck. A lot of Dutch people didn't like my opponent, who I believe was a doorman, and they were saying, 'I hope you knock him out.' On the day of the fight, I was thinking, as I always do, *Yeah, I can do this. I can beat him with my stamina.*

I came out to the ring first: strutting my stuff, music playing, feeling sweet. He came out and I thought, *Yeah*. He was staring at me and I was staring at him. The ref told us to come together and touch gloves. I don't think we did, I just turned around and walked back to my corner. The crowd were going, 'Ooh!'

Then I came out and started beating fuck out of the guy. Within the first minute of the first round, I gave him a cut across his eye. The referee stopped the fight for about two minutes just to attend to this one fucking cut! I thought, *Why stop the fight? Just wipe the blood away!* The crowd were going mad and it was all action till the end of the first round. There was blood streaming down his face.

I think I just about pinched the round.

In the second round, we were on the floor, till the ref stood us up. I threw a right hand at him and Kasteel moved out of the way. He turned and caught me right in the temple. My legs buckled and I dropped to the floor. I managed to crawl to the ropes and pull myself up. When the ref asked if I was all right, I shook my head, but I still said, 'Yeah.'

He gave me a standing count and asked if I still wanted to fight. 'Yeah!' I could hear Dev and everyone shouting, 'Come on, Barrington, come on, Barrington!'

I took one step forward and we were at it again. We were both on the floor and he had me in a scarf hold. No one taps out of a scarf hold but my head was still fucked with dizziness. I was dizzy, dizzy, dizzy! I was lying there and I couldn't do anything. I was fucked, man!

So I tapped out and that was it. I lost the fight; he put his hands up and we embraced each other. The crowd were going fucking wild!

But I'd been banging him till the ref stopped the fight to attend to his cut. It gave him two full minutes to recuperate. Still, it was a great fight all the way, with two great big lumps having it off. But when I got back to the changing room I just buried my head in my hands. I thought, *The ref's a wanker, they're all fucking wankers!* I'd put on such a good show.

The promoter said, 'The crowd want you to fight again.' It was nice for me, having come from England to fight someone on their own manor. I wish I'd been around in Roman days because I would have been a gladiator. I'd have boxed some people up.

I'd fought my heart out and lost, but still – I'd fought my heart out. The promoter said I'd always entertained the crowd and they came first. So, if the promoter was happy, I was happy.

But it felt horrible to lose that fight. I felt cheated and frustrated with the ref for stopping the fight for two minutes to attend to a fucking cut! He shouldn't have stopped it; he should have put some Vaseline on the cut and carried on. The break gave the guy a chance to get his oxygen back. At the end of the day, I wasn't badly injured and I moved on to the next fight. Kasteel and me had a little chat at the after party. He was another Dutch guy, and all of my fights had been with guys from the same camp so far.

My next fight was a big one and he was a *cunt*! He was a doorman and this fight was hyped up to the fucking max. There were massive posters on billboards in Amsterdam, in surrounding areas and at the airport too.

Now I was actually one of the top fighters. My training was spot on and everything was going great for me, but none of the other Dutch fighters wanted to know. It was only the ones from MMA trainer Chris Dolman's gym who all wanted a pop at me.

The fight was with a guy called Dick Vrij (pronounced 'Vry'). He was from the same camp and he was a hard fucker too, a real lunatic. I trained for six solid weeks with a couple of boxers, one of whom was Rob M. Norton from Stourbridge. I worked with the boxers to get my hands working again. My grappling and my stand-up were second to none, and my kicking was unbelievable! Everything was worked to a 'T'.

I left on the Friday as usual with Andre, Dev and Mattie Evans. Everyone was in a good mood when we arrived in Holland. But at the Saturday press conferences and weigh-in, I looked at Vrij and he looked fucking evil! He was only about two or three inches taller than me but he was an evil motherfucker. I think we weighed about the same, as I weighed 17 stone, 5 pounds – my fighting weight. (When I wasn't fighting, I weighed about 18 stone.)

DEV

They wouldn't let Barrington and him weigh-in in the same room. They were hostile. Dick Vrij is one of these characters who takes everything really seriously. It gets him in a lot of fights. Barrington was showboating and he took it funny. They said there probably would have been a fight before the fight, so they made sure they didn't meet until they got in the ring.

That was a big fight. I think it's probably one of the biggest they've ever held, 20- to 30-odd thousand people were there. It was held at the Amsterdam Arena. He was fighting in memory of his dad who died from cancer, and I was just fighting because it was a fight.

On the day, when I came out of the changing room, I thought, *I've got a fucking hard fight on my hands, three five-minute rounds.* I came out and did all the normal stuff I do. He came out and the crowd went fucking wild – I mean *wild, wild, wild!* I was standing in the ring and there was fucking tinsel coming out of the sky – even though, before the fight, not a lot of people liked him because they said he's a doorman, he's a bully. So people were going beforehand, 'I hope you beat him!' 'Kick his arse!' and things like that. But when it came to the reception, when he came out it was *unbelievable.*

We came out in the centre of the ring and squared up to each other. I was staring at him and thinking, *Yeah, we're gonna have a right tear-up!* He was a standing fighter like me. He didn't want to go to the ground and nor did I. In the first round, he had me on the back foot a couple of times, up against the ropes. He was kicking the shit out of me and I just stood there.

I'm sure the referee ended that fight because, even though I was up for it, Vrij was better than me. So I was there giving it my all, I was fighting, but he had me up against the ropes for 30 seconds, kicking, punching. I wasn't throwing anything back. I just couldn't – I probably put too much into the first round. It was one of those fights where somebody had to go down.

It only lasted two rounds. But it was a proper tear-up, a punishing fight. I came back from Holland in a wheelchair. I couldn't walk for two or three days.

* * *

Then the promoter set me up with a guy called Dave Dalgliesh. I never change my tactics; I carry on with the same thing. Like Dev said, 'Just do what you normally do.'

Dalgliesh was about a stone and a half lighter than me. He's another Dutch guy and had even more experience than the last fighter, but I watched the DVDs of him fighting and thought, *I'll fucking eat this cunt!* He was younger than me, in his twenties, and his stand-up wasn't that good – but he was brilliant on the floor. I thought I'd carry on doing the same old things, but this was a big fight and I needed a win to get myself back up there again. I was a big scalp for opponents and with two losses under my belt I needed this one. I wanted to get back up there again. I watched the DVDs and I trained, trained, trained fucking hard!

I got to Holland and it was the same shit as usual: I stood with him at press conferences and had pictures taken. We were talking to each other and everything was nice. He even said, 'Thanks for giving me the opportunity,' and I answered, 'Yeah, no problem at all.'

Everything had gone to plan: my coaches and trainers were there; people came over from Birmingham to watch. Everything seemed the same as usual. When I came out to the ring and we looked at each other, I thought, *You're mine, you're mine*. Then he came out, grabbed my legs and got me on the floor.

He's tied me up and I'm thinking, *Fucking hell!* He's on top of me and pounding me! *How do I get out of these fucking moves?* I didn't expect this to happen at all. I'm trying to punch him off but I can't. He's just raining punches down on top of me and I'm thinking, *What the fuck do I do now?* He was lighter than me and I'd really underestimated him. Mattie is shouting 'Do this!' and 'Do that!'

And I'm trying to do this and that but nothing's fucking happening! The referee shouts, 'Get back out there!' Dalgliesh hits me with a combination and he's pounding me on the floor. I'm trying to cover up and turn the guy but he's turned me and got me back in position. He's punching and pounding me, and then the fight is over! Good referee.

DEV

Barrington is now going into a world where these guys have been fighting a long time. It's a totally different thing, so that's where the struggle was. You need maturity in this sport. Those guys were top pros, they were like our pro boxers in England. They were fighting regularly, all of them. Barrington was just a guy who was having a go at it, so he was up against people that in reality he shouldn't have been fighting. He was a fish out of water really.

The mistake I really made is that I should have taken more fights. Even fights over here. I was just relying on one fight a year: the big one in Holland. So all these guys that I fought in MMA were far more experienced than I was. If I had one fight they'd probably had eight or nine or 15 fights. So there were lots of mistakes I made: I should have got more fights behind me and got the experience, but I thought, *Why fight over here and get your teeth kicked out?* But that's how I learned.

It was a foreign sport. But, like the guy says, they were all more experienced than I was, every single one of 'em. But I was just blessed with someone to fight. To actually come up against people who were better than me. Even though some of them were more experienced than me, I still took them on.

After that fight, I really started to improve my groundwork. There was no doubt that Dalgliesh was a brilliant fighter. The crowd went fucking wild, but after the fight he came up and thanked me.

So it was back to the drawing board. *It's not the end of the world*, I told myself. MMA is a really short career though, and it was much too late for me to switch over to boxing.

CHAPTER TWELVE

In 2005, a local promoter called Dean Griffiths of Cage Warriors asked me if I wanted to fight in Coventry. I thought, *Well it's my own manor, so yeah*. It was against Emmanuel Marc from France, who'd had X amount of fights and was more of a grappler than me. It was a massive fight and it was the first time that it wasn't with Showtime, which was one of the biggest organisations promoting MMA in Holland at the time.

DEV

Back at the beginning, when Barrington went down south in Holland, they all wanted him – the main promoter, Simon Rutz, later described Barrington as being the fighter that made the phrase 'It's Showtime!' He got involved with Showtime and that was it. Because normally, when you get to a top organisation like that, when you lose once they won't have you back. But they had Barrington back.

I'd had a bit of a setback and had fallen out with my missus. But at the same time I wanted to entertain the crowd and to win in Coventry. About 60 or 70 Blues lads turned up; they'd obviously heard that the Coventry Legion were going to be there, so I warned everyone and told them they'd better get their doors sorted out. I warned the doormen there would be trouble but they said, 'Nah, it's gonna be all right.'

I was having a big fight in Coventry and it was on my manor, so I also asked my dad, who was now living in Wisbech, Cambridgeshire, to come and watch. It was the first time he'd ever watched me fight and he came with his wife, Colleen. I got them picked up by one of my friends, Alana, who brought them from the hotel. (My mum had never come to watch since she saw me fight a couple of years ago, when I won the Midland Area Title in Wolver-hampton – so this was my dad's time.) Even when I was banged up for months in a borstal, I wouldn't ring him and tell my dad I was in jail or anything like that. I just didn't want to tell him. But he knew when I was fighting – he didn't mind because he was coming from the same place as me. He'd heard about me fighting and seen DVDs – but he'd never actually seen me fight and he loved his fighting, his martial arts and boxing.

Lucy, my girlfriend at the time, and my two daughters were there too: Leonie, who's now 25, and Bailey, who's now 18. The SkyDome Arena was a sell-out – no seats left at all! As I came into the stadium with Andre and Dev, chatting with a couple of mates from Birmingham and Coventry, the atmosphere was just fucking electric!

ANDRE

Barrington is fiercely protective of his family and close friends. There was an incident where I had to pull him off a guy. This was when we were driving around checking on door staff; I got a call from a pub where Baz's daughter was working and a guy had put his hand up her skirt. This is probably the most angry I have ever seen him and it was all over in about 15 seconds. Baz absolutely destroyed this guy, to the point where I had to stop him for his own good. (Trust me, he looked like he had gone through a windscreen; he was a mess.) That was scary, but two minutes later he was laughing and joking again like nothing had happened.

I went backstage and started warming up for the fight. People kept trying to ask if I was OK but I wanted to be on my own. The last thing I want to hear is people coming in and saying, 'Hope you win.' Don't *hope* – I'm going to win, I am *going to* fucking win!

Training up to the fight had gone well. It was on a Saturday night. My fight was the last of the night, billed as the main event. Marc came out first. When I came out in my Birmingham City top, with 'Zulu' written on the back, the crowd gave a big roar. All I heard was 'ZULU!' from the Blues lads situated behind the VIP area. Everyone rushed towards the fence and hung on it; security couldn't do a thing about it. The crowd were going wild!

The place was chock-a-block. At one stage, the MC for the night had to come to the mic and say, 'Can you all move back from the stage please?' Most of my friends had tickets for outside of the VIP area – they just pushed the security out of the way and walked into it.

When it all calmed down, the referee called us to the centre of the ring. He gave us a few instructions and then it was 'FIGHT!'

I came out feeling sharp. I felt wicked! I had him up against the cage. I was picking him off, jabbing him, kicking him, jabbing him, kicking him . . .

Then, all of a sudden, I got up too close to him, like a twat! My plan was to stay away from him and fight him on the outside, but he turned me, suplexed me and got me to the floor. I then turned him over and the ref stood us up. We carried on fighting. He shot forward at me and knocked me back on the floor. The guy was just bashing me, beating the head off me, and I was trying to block him.

All of a sudden, he stopped punching. He just sat on me and looked up. I had my hands on my head and all I saw was the ref walking over. Marc had stopped punching me so I thought, *I'll put my hands down now*, but the ref said, 'Carry on fighting.' Then the guy just went *BANG!*

I was out cold. That's all I remember. Apparently I was out for about three minutes.

All the Zulus smashed the fucking place up! The riot police came in and then ran out again. When I came around, I took the microphone, telling the crowd, 'Please stop, please stop!' My dad, step-mum and daughters had to run and hide. Apparently, four or five of the main Blues lads were stood back to back, just banging any fucker in sight that didn't appear to be from Birmingham. At one stage, they even tried to hit Rupert, my best Brummie friend!

All I can remember is I came round at the side, I stood up and there were just chairs all over the place. Apparently, Alana got my step-mum and my dad out and took them back to the hotel. They were seated right at the front of the cage but I found out afterwards there was loads of trouble: bottles and chairs were flying everywhere, so Alana made sure they were safe.

MAL

It was the fight against this French guy in the Coventry SkyDome Arena and it was a night to remember; it kicked off big-time. It was after I'd met back up with Barrington and asked him what he was doing; he said, 'Cage fighting – I'll get tickets for ya.' I said, 'No problem, but I've got about 15 guys with me.'

When we went out, everyone knew Barrington, and on this particular night we didn't have to queue up anywhere; we went straight to the front and they said, 'Here you go, Baz.' It was amazing; it was like being a celebrity! (This was in Brum at the Hyatt hotel in 2000. He got me involved at the place where he was training in Coventry and told them to look after me.)

Basically, we knew it was going to be a good night. But there were a lot of people in Birmingham who didn't like people from Coventry. There was even this copper there, an inspector, and he said, 'Are you sure about this? It's going to kick off tonight.' And I was going, 'Nah, nah,' because I was excited! So we met at my house about seven o'clock and everyone was talking about how it was going to kick off down there because of what this inspector said, but I was saying no.

We got there and you could see there was tension straight away. There were a couple of groups standing about and no one was standing near them; everyone else was just queuing away from that area. Barrington got me a VIP ticket but the other lads were sitting at the top of the arena, so I was separated from them.

It did kick off at the back as well, but I wasn't there; I was on a table with Barrington's daughter and some other guys I used to train with just a step away from the ring. I could see Barrington waving at me and he was really ready for it.

Further back there was a guy in a white shirt and he

was kicking off a bit. There was a table of Zulus and they were just looking at him. People were trying to get this guy to sit down. I remember he had a white shirt on, because by the end of the evening it was red. I'm not joking!

Now I kept saying it was going to kick off and other people at the table were saying, 'It'll be all right.' But I knew those guys wanted to kill each other. It was like a football match and they were all shouting, 'Zulu! Zulu!'

Then Barrington's fight started and he came out in this big Zulu top. The French guy came out and the guy with the mic introduced Barrington. After that you couldn't hear the other guy's name!

The guy in the white shirt was still standing up and I thought, 'He's going to get killed.' You could feel the tension. People were walking around with bottles in their hands, looking across at each other, and I'm sat right in the middle of it!

The fight went off. What happened was there was so much noise going on that the ref called a stop for the end of the round and this guy kept going, hitting Barrington on the back of the head. People were just running towards the ring, I thought they were going to rip the cage apart!

Barrington had stopped fighting because he thought the round was over. He was knocked out and this other guy was declared the winner. These guys were surrounding the ring, throwing bottles and spitting and everything. Next thing you know, this guy with the white shirt gets involved and they steam in and kick the absolute shit out of him; they were waiting to do him anyway, it was just a matter of time. Then there were chairs flying across, tables flying across, cans, bottles, glasses, you name it, but there was no security at all. They just ran out!

It was such an electric atmosphere; there were so many tables and chairs flying across that it was like a war zone! Just two sets of blokes smashing into each other, Coventry and Birmingham, with a nervous lot in the middle. The guy in the white shirt was asking for a kicking anyway. There were pockets that no one wanted to stand next to; there were some people who were just there for a little night out with the wife and they were looking around the place in amazement. It was like a bomb had hit it.

Barrington had got up by now and told them to stop it and to calm down, but they weren't listening. You could see that the guy in the white shirt's face had dropped off. His nose was red, his face was red; they took him away. Oh my God! All I could see was 30 boys running from one side to the other and it just kicked off big-time; there were chairs and tables going everywhere. The police didn't come in until the lads had kicked the shit out of everyone. They knew the Zulus were there and they didn't want to come in until they'd tired themselves out from fighting! They were expecting it, so the inspector *told me. His division were outside. He was sat as part of my group but he was in the top tier – he was safe. There were chairs flying over my head, I'd never seen anything like it. It was exciting though!*

One of Barrington's daughters nearly got knocked out, so I took her to the side and got her out of there. She would only have been 16 or 17 and she was really upset about it. But it was a fantastic night; we still talk about it now because there's a guy who lives in Worcester who comes down and he jokes: 'I'm never going to go out with you again! If I'm out with you lot, then there's going to be a fight.' We were at this Ricky Hatton after-dinner thing in the Holiday Inn and some guy got bottled there when it kicked off. This guy goes: 'Wherever you and Barrington are, there's always a fight! Trouble follows you wherever you go!' I'll never forget that night in Coventry; it's like part of local folklore.

Everything had gone out of the window, but it still takes a man to step into the cage. I know they can battle it out on the streets, but out of all the guys that were there only two of us could actually get in the cage and fight.

It was mayhem. The police had to come in with dogs. All the chairs and tables were turned upside down. After this, I said, 'I've had enough now.' I was near enough 40 and I'd been there and done it all. I went back to my changing room and cried like a fucking baby for about five fucking minutes! Dev always said to me, 'You never stop till the ref says stop.' But I'd put my hands down like a twat and got punished for it.

My dad stayed around to make sure I was all right after the fight. I don't think I spoke to him till the day after, when he left to go home to Wisbech. He was saying that he thought the guy had killed me, that I'd died in the ring and things like that. He was shook up, it was emotional for him.

It was the first time I'd been knocked out in my life – even on the street. I'd lost in front of my own crowd and in front of my dad, who was there supporting me. But he was proud because he'd seen some fighters and because of the amount of people who were there supporting me.

When I first started fighting, I always said to myself, *The day I get knocked out is the day I call it a day.* But I still wanted to carry on.

I went home after that and sat on my own. I cried like a fucking bitch: *I can't believe I've been beaten in front of all these people; I've never been knocked out.* But the hardest part was going back to the gym and getting back in the cage or ring to fight again.

I knew I wasn't invincible, but I just couldn't believe I'd been knocked out. Eventually, I had to come out and face people in Coventry. I had people saying to me, 'You got knocked out!' on my Facebook page. But so what if I got fucking knocked out?

It was hard walking down the street. Even though I was there for the fight, there are a lot of people in Coventry who fucking hate me anyway, and a lot of people want to see me get knocked out, lose or get beaten up. It was hard walking around the town, but I just held my head up high and thought, *Fuck it! You can all talk outside the ring, get in the ring and do it your fucking self!* And half of those fuckers can't. Most sat there and talked: 'He should have done this, he should have done that' – you go and do it.

'Ain't it about time you finished now? You're getting old now' – that's all I used to get off my mum and my step-mum.

'Do what you wanna do' – that's what my dad said.

Dev said, 'If you wanna carry on fighting, carry on fighting.'

When I first started fighting, I just wanted to fight. I didn't give a fuck about the money or whatever, I didn't care if you were a fighter or a world champion – I'd fight you. But later on the money got hold of it: I wasn't fighting for the fight; I was fighting for the money. And that's one of the things that really got me in the end. I wasn't fighting because I wanted to hurt someone or whatever; I thought, *I could earn six or seven grand 'ere.*

But fuck that, I just wanted to fight! I get in the ring, I'm a gladiator: I'm a human being, you're a human being – it's who's got the better heart at the end of the day. I saw my opponent as a stepping stone for me.

What was going through my mind was: *I've lost the fight and all I can do is pick myself up. It's back to the drawing board again.* But I knew I'd fought a better fight, even though I'd lost, because all the promoters around the country wanted me to fight in their shows! So I knew there were bigger fish to fry. Why? Because I'm a fighter and an entertainer!

But I needed a bit of time to think. It was two weeks after that before I even got back to the gym, to tell the truth. I thought, *I'm not ready to retire yet; I'm not ready to finish yet. I shouldn't let one knockout stop me from fighting again. I know I can progress and go further. I want to go again. I can carry on, I can go again.* It was pure frustration: *I know I can do better than what I'm doing and I can carry on fighting. I've still got a couple of fights left in me.*

I told Dev that I'd achieved what I wanted to achieve and I'd had enough. 'I'm gonna call it a day. I've got a world title in kickboxing. I've won the British, European, Intercontinental and Midland Area titles, I've won every kickboxing title going. I've had a long run and I've done fucking good. But . . . I'd like one more fight.'

MAL

It didn't bother him at all; he was beating a lot of people, he would never walk away from a fight. I think there were only two clubs in Coventry where the bouncers would actually go near him; he came to my son's 18th and the bouncers were terrified of him! I said to my son, 'I hope everyone's happy here, mate, because they don't want to be kicking off!' His physical presence on the door was enough.

BARRINGTON PATTERSON

Everywhere I'd go with Barrington, someone knew him; he'd go to New York and get treated like a king, staying in a five-star hotel.

His last fight before he retired was with a Dutch guy and it was amazing: Rob Schreiber. Good fight.

Above: After defeating Big Mo T, the referee put my hand in the air and said, 'The winner, Barrington "Zulu" Patterson!'

Above: Joop Kasteel: 'Kasteel' means 'castle' and he is built like a castle.

Right: Action in the ring: giving the audience a real show for their money, fighting against a Dutch kickboxer for an IKKC title.

Left: Andre has been in my corner at most of my fights and he pushes me hard. He'll say, 'Come on Baz, come on Baz, you gotta do it!'

Above: I've always walked out to the same song playing – 'Walk like a Champion' by Buju Banton – throughout my whole career.

Left: Cage Warriors asked me if I wanted to fight in Coventry. I thought, *Well it's my own manor, so yeah.*

Right: My dad, Karl, at the only fight he attended.

Right: What was going through my mind was: I've lost the fight and all I can do is pick myself up. It's back to the drawing board again.

Right: All the Zulus smashed the place up! The riot police came in and then ran out again.

Left: I'd fought the promoter Henk Kuiper twice, the first time at kyokushin karate; he later offered me my dream fight against Bob Schreiber.

Right: For my final fight, I agreed to be filmed for the TV series *Danny Dyer's Deadliest Men*.

Left: I was fighting Dutch legend Bob Schreiber for the world title – billed as 'King the Ring'.

ES!' I'd finally done it; I'd got my belt and I couldn't wait to put it around my waist when ey announced me as World Champion.

Left: Leeds at home; West Ham at home; Millwall away; Villa always: the Zulus have a firm to reckon with.

Right: Terry, Rupert, Todd and me (left to right): very close friends for life.

Left: Dynamo Zagreb's firm, the Bad Blue Boys, invited us to watch a game on their turf.

Right: A firm of us flew to Croatia for the Maribor (Slovenia) v Birmingham City game.

Left: Rupert, me, Todd, Andre and Eves (left to right); Adam and Jeff (foreground).

Right: Author Cass Pennant and I meeting my old friends Kam and Patty, in Handsworth.

Right: Buster's arm, Sharkey, Lewis, Bajey and Curly – Original Tiger Posse (left to right).

Left: In 2012 I asked my Tracey to marry me. To m surprise, she said YES.

Right: I look ahead but I don't plan things – I just live from day to day.

CHAPTER THIRTEEN

This promoter, Henk Kuipers from Holland, rang me out of the blue in 2008 when I was in bed. He was also a good fighter and I'd fought him twice, the first time in one of the hardest forms of knockdown karate. At that time, I didn't know anything about it at all, so I'd gone to Geoff Thompson, borrowed a book and watched some videos. At the time, he was the top fighter in Holland and I beat him at his own sport. Then I fought him again 14 years later and everyone says I won it, but they gave it to him. It was no problem.

There was only one person I wanted to fight before I retired. Bob Schreiber was originally from the same Dutch camp but he'd gone off and done his own thing. I'd known Schreiber for over 10 years and that's who I wanted to make my money from for this last fight. At the time, he'd also retired. So when the promoter said, 'I'll pay you 20,000 Euros if you want to fight Schreiber,' I cut him short right there: 'Damn fucking right I'll fight him!'

Bob Schreiber was one of the most respected fighters in Holland. He'd been around for years and had fought Wanderlei Silva and the real top dogs. I told Dev, 'I want one last fight and that's the person I'm gonna fight.' Plus, from day one, when I met him he was always such a nice guy. I watched his fights and DVDs and what a fighter; he was just unbelievable. He'd fought all these guys around the world. So it was an honour for me for him just to say, 'Yeah, I'm fighting Barrington Patterson.'

I'd earned enough respect in my life and I wanted this one last fight – but when the promoter said about the money I was dancing about for over a week, just thinking about the 20,000 Euros. There was no negotiation on the purse offered. Like a twat I just said yes, lying on the sofa half-asleep and dreaming about my biggest ever earnings. I didn't think to say, 'I should talk to my manager first,' who'd be unlikely to take the first offer as he'd figure Schreiber would be on 40,000–50,000 Euros. We may have got it closer to 30,000 Euros and when I told Dev he said, 'Why the bloody hell did you say yes?' The line of thought was that my popularity with the Dutch fanbase hadn't waned, even though it'd been four years since the Dalgliesh fight with rival Dutch promoters Showtime.

But it didn't matter. I'd got the big payday I'd sought for my retirement fight and I was buzzing. At the end of the day, 20,000 Euros was a lot of money in this sport and I couldn't wait to get into my training.

DEV

From very early on in the fights – whether you're fighting in the pure karate or the contact, which is championship level – it doesn't matter what level you are, from your very first fight to your last fight you have to have somebody to look after you from day one. You cannot fight without someone who is responsible for your safety, and that's from the word go. But obviously, once you get to the big fights and negotiating money that's a different thing.

I was living in Leamington Spa at the time with my missus Lucy, son and stepdaughter. I'd be getting up at 6am and returning home about 10pm; the kids would be in bed, she was in bed, so I'd make myself something to eat, have a shower, go to bed and get up early in the morning while everyone else was still in bed – then go to the gym, go to work and continue the training in Holland at the weekends. I'd even got myself a personal trainer who used to play rugby for England, so I was training properly for the most important fight of my career.

I was training for an hour at a time four times a day, for five to six days a week. My first training session would start at 6am, then I'd split up the rest of the day. One day, I'd be doing weight training in the morning, then I'd probably go out on a run followed by a boxing lesson; then it was kickboxing the next day, followed a couple of hours later by a jiu-jitsu lesson and then a grappling lesson. I just kept on mixing it up every day with a jog or a bit of running, mostly hill sprints.

(I got that routine from rugby, which I didn't start playing until I was 36. I played recently and we lost, but two of their guys got stretchered off so I'd done my job. I like contact sports. I guess I've been lucky with injuries – nothing in rugby and just broken hands and thumbs in kickboxing. When I broke my thumb in a fight in Coventry I'd gone five rounds, but it wasn't until four days later that my girlfriend noticed the palm of my hand had gone black. I went up to the hospital where they told me I'd broken two bones in my thumb.)

I never saw the effect all this was having on my family because I wasn't seeing the kids. The missus and me were always arguing because I was focused totally on this fight. Then came the bombshell: she wanted to split up after another argument, so I moved out and ended up sleeping on my mate's settee. I couldn't see my son and I still had this big fight looming; my head was becoming messed up.

In the middle of all this, I went to watch an Ian Freeman fight at the NEC and was sitting in the audience when I was approached by a guy who said he was from ZigZag Productions: 'We know all about you and we really want to do a documentary on you.'

'Who, *me*?'

So now I've agreed to do this documentary while still training for my last big fight, in a situation where I've moved out of the house and I'm going through shit with my now ex-missus. I've always had more than one girl on the go at a time: I was probably seeing five or six girls, but I was going through loads of shit with Lucy, I couldn't see my kids and I ended up in trouble with the police again over her. Lucy had given me a nice little son, Kye – that's the one on the Danny Dyer documentary with the curly hair, who's now eight years old. (I also have another son, Tyler, who's nearly eight.) I ended up with Lucy but we didn't get married, I just lived with her for about five or six years. Things didn't work out right – I ended up catching her out as well and got in trouble with the police for what I did to her. I hammered her. I ended up in court for that one.

Domestic problems – no matter how big you are, man, they'll get you! As they say, a small axe will chop down a big tree. That's what was happening.

I was getting no sleep, I was taking too much on and I wasn't dealing with it all; one thing was leading to another. I was now some three or four weeks from the fight and clearly not coping, so I went to the doctor who put me on antidepressants and sleeping tablets. I was starting to lose it; I was sleeping on a mate's settee and things like that.

DEV

You could see it was getting to him, and the way he was going on I could actually see that perhaps he was going to end up doing something he would regret. So obviously I had to sit down with him and have a good chat about life and things: 'You've done all this, look at what you've achieved, why do you wanna throw it all away? At this moment, you can do something about it.' I think it was more about those things that were going on: he had to take a look at what he was doing, a look at himself. Then there was the situation with Lucy: 'You've got your kids – how can you throw all that away as well?' I think he listened.

That was the second one where I gave evidence and there was another funny incident: Barrington was back behind bars and I went to see him, chatting about things. And he started telling me the truth about things that had happened, telling me about all the bad things that I didn't know he had done. There was a time when some guys had got locked up on the ferry from Holland. They'd found ganja. At this point, four years later, it's like he's confessing to all the things he's done before they put him away: 'Remember that time we were coming home? Remember that ganja that was found? That was mine.' Maybe it was prison that was making him confess to all those things.

Since I've known Dev, I've been through quite a few

women – my wives and ex-girlfriends and people like that. So it wasn't the first time I'd been in a situation where he's helped me. I couldn't go into a fight with a dangerous opponent in the frame of mind I was in; my preparation had to be right for a sport like this. So I pleaded with my missus, 'Even if we ain't getting on, let me back to sleep in my son's room.' I needed a bit of home comfort, to come home and see my kids. I'd given up my flat to move in with her, so if she said no it was back to my mate's settee. But she said no, no, no.

I went back to my trainer and simply said, 'I can't fight, I don't want to fight. My head's not there, it just ain't gonna happen with me.' I don't think Dev was surprised by what I was confessing. I was taking the odd liberty too, and Dev had to pull me aside after one such liberty and tell me, in a fatherly fashion, that I couldn't keep going on like this, with all these women doing my head in all the time. Things had got to the stage where I'd be training and sparring with people and be so pissed off and moody that I'd knock them out.

The documentary we were making was being presented by the actor Danny Dyer. I told him, 'I've got this last fight coming up,' and he said they wanted to come to Holland and record it. I said, 'My missus has now agreed we can come back to film at the house, but I'm still not allowed to bloody stay there!'

About two weeks before the fight, I did manage to get back with her; she then asked to come and watch me. I said, 'No. You knew how important this was to me; you knew how hard I'd have to prepare for this.' I couldn't have my head messed with again. But I was happy enough to be back in the house, to be around my son, my step-daughter and my missus.

And I knew deep down that I was hungry for it. I really wanted this fight; this was my chance to be a world champion. I'd always wanted to be a champion, no matter if it was kickboxing or karate or Mixed Martial Arts. I'd said to myself, *Whenever I get to win the world title, that's it for me: end of story, dream achieved.*

At Amsterdam's Schiphol Airport, there was an impressive crowd of people waiting as soon as I got off the plane. My fight had captured the imagination of the people – this was a big, *big* billing. He was one of Holland's most famous fighters and he was coming out of retirement to fight me just as I was going into retirement.

They booked a hotel in Rotterdam for me and all my friends from Coventry. Dev was flying over the next day, more friends were staying in Amsterdam and, from the calls we were getting, we knew that more were arriving later. So I said, 'Fuck it, let's all have a Friday night out in Amsterdam!' We found a cool bar and it was nice; I sat back in my chair looking around the bar. All my important friends were there, smoking the weed, drinking, dancing, talking and just enjoying themselves. They'd all come to see me fight.

Dev said be in bed by midnight, but I ended up staying

in another hotel I'd checked myself into after sampling the Amsterdam nightlife. It was four in the morning before we all got back, then I had to go to Rotterdam in a few hours. Even then, more friends were arriving and texting me to ask me to join them, but I knew the night before had been enough for me. I was content in a nice hotel just a half-hour away from the venue. I went out for something to eat with my group of friends, checked back in the afternoon and tried out the big Jacuzzi before going back out on the port town that is Rotterdam. Then Dev turned up: 'Barrington, make sure you're in by 12 o'clock!' Sorry, Dev, but this is my time. I never hit the bed until about four in the morning again. *Hee, hee!*

When I woke up that Sunday morning, everything felt unreal. I had to remind myself I was fighting for the world title – to become what they billed as 'King of the Rings'. I went down to have breakfast and went out for a walk. Then two o'clock struck and we were due at the stadium for half past two.

When I was taken to the fight venue, I was feeling on top. I'd never felt like this before. People were coming up to me all the time, shaking hands and asking for autographs in the build-up to the fight. It was to take place at the Ahoy, an indoor arena most famous for large-scale pop concerts. The show was sold out in advance, the place packed with thousands of people. It was even going to be shown live on the net. I was there in the middle of the afternoon and my fight was the top of the bill, so I was on a high with time on my hands, which I used to wander around the stadium and mingle with people. 'Hey, Patterson!' some of them would call out in recognition.

I just couldn't believe I was finally fighting Bob Schreiber. There were four other fighters in the changing room I was sharing, which was fully kitted out with fruit, food, water and even a TV – everything you might want. As I got warmed up, it seemed like everyone just stopped what they were doing and watched me. I had people walking in and out, saying something in Dutch that means 'success' or 'good luck'. There were TV cameras there for the fight build-up, and the Danny Dyer film crew were filming every step I took for the documentary. I also had about 30 or 40 people come over from Coventry and Birmingham to watch the fight.

Then came the time to walk down the stairs and make my big ring entrance. I thought I'd milk it for all its worth; it was my time. As 'Walk like a Champion' came on, it was time to do my strut behind my two dancing girls. Everyone was jumping out of their seats, making noise, and I was just lapping it all up. I had my Blues football shirt on and my dark glasses; as I got into the ring, the music stopped and it was his turn to come out – my opponent.

The place erupted when he came out and did his little thing – but you can't showboat a showboater! I can't remember the music he came out to but it goes something like 'Mother-*fuckerrrs!*' and he came out with his hands up in the air. The crowd just went mad. We even had those small heater things with flames at the side. There were more than 20,000 people there at the Ahoy stadium, it was live on the Internet and live on TV. When he came out he was just electrifying.

As we climbed into the ring and shook hands, the ref got into the middle and said, 'Fighters get ready . . .'

DEV

Schreiber has got that way where he pulls both hands up in the air and stands there, and that look on his face is like Robbie Williams! I think Robbie Williams must have got it from him, because he holds his hands up, gives that look and just sort of turns slowly over to the side of the crowd. That's him. But he's a great fighter, he really is.

Now it was time. I ran out into him – jab left leg – jab right leg – jab left leg again – and when I hit him with my right hand he stumbled. I thought, *I ain't going to make the mistake of rushing in to finish him off. Nah, I'm going to pace myself.* I knew this Dutch legend was a durable guy and he could really bang. But at this stage I was more than pleased with myself as I was knocking him all over the place; I was giving him some big hits and keeping him on the back foot all the time.

Fair play to him though, because at one time he had me on the ropes and was bashing me as I struggled to get away. So I stood off the ropes, looked at him and punched him straight back. Back he went and then I had him on the floor. I mounted him and started to pummel him with blows to end the first round.

DEV

Andre was in the corner with me when I remember saying to Barrington at the end of the third, 'Why did you let him off?' because he put him down and he could have finished him off. I was cursing him! I said, 'You've done that before, Barrington – let somebody off when you got sleepy. It's happened again! Why are you backing off?' Because he had him out and he stood back. He has done that in a lot of fights – he's had people going, and he's just backed off. So in the second round that's all I kept saying to him.

In the second round, he had me up against the ropes and he was like *BOOM! BOOM!* and I had my head covered. And, all of a sudden, I just poked my head up and laughed at him, and hit him with a right hand!

Then I let him off. I don't know why – it's just me. Maybe I want 'em to soak up some more punishment.

I sat back down in my corner, Dev said to me, 'Take yer time, man, you can beat this guy.'

'It stands out a mile that I can beat this guy!' I cut in.

Then I went out for the second round and continued in the same manner as I finished the first. A couple of times he had me on the back foot until we stood facing each other, punching the shit out of one another. It was becoming a proper stand-up fight and the crowd were erupting as we traded blow for blow and kick for kick. I was spitting out blood through my gum shield; he had cuts and big bruises on his leg.

In the third and final round, we continued our out-and-out war, banging each other to fuck. I was feeling grateful that I was in the best shape I'd been in for any fight.

At the end of the round, Dev said, 'You've got it, you've got it!' I just thought, *Dev, you're not remembering that most times, in order to beat these guys on their own patch, you've got to knock the mothers out.*

We stood out in the centre of the ring as the ref announced, 'The winner, Barrington "Zulu" Patterson!'

I fell down on my knees screaming, 'YES!' I'd finally done it; I'd got my belt and I couldn't wait to put it around my waist when they announced me as World Champion. Bob gallantly said, 'Well done and thanks for giving me the fight.'

Dev was in the ring and all my other friends were climbing in. It was unreal, it just seemed like everyone was in there with me.

ANDRE

Baz and I have not only worked together but we also trained together; this involved punching each other in the face. Sparring regularly with Baz is great if you don't mind an 18-stone guy trying to knock your head off or kicking you in the head and then fighting you on the floor. I used to train him on boxing skills for all his fights. I would sort out his striking and his fitness. Baz used to hate me at this point because I put him through hell to get him fit. I did his corner all over the world and I was there when he won the world MMA title against the legendry Bob Schreiber. What a fight! He beat him in his own backyard in Holland and that was the highlight of Barrington's career. It was an honour to be there with him.

When I sat back down in the changing room I was covered in blood. All of my mouth was bleeding and I had bruises everywhere, but, hey, I was 20,000 Euros better off and I was the World Champion. The cameras rolled on me and I said, 'This is it: finished, Alpha–Omega, the beginning and the end.' I'd finished on top.

DEV
They were both towards the end of their career. We had a rules meeting and 'spinning back-fist' was banned – it's really dangerous, instead of hitting them with your fist you end up hitting them with your elbow in the forearm. It's not only a knockout; it does a lot of damage. So we had a little set-to about that at the rules meeting and his wife – who's a fighter as well, she's probably as big as him – was the one who was arguing with us about it. I've looked at Schreiber and I've watched him fight. Some of

the cleanest knockouts that I've ever seen are from Bob Schreiber. To go into a ring with a legend like that is something special – let alone to have beaten him.

Two years before that, if they'd have said, 'I want Barrington to fight him,' I'd have said, 'No way,' because Barrington wasn't experienced enough for Schreiber then. But I thought he had it at that time, and, although they say he came out of retirement, he didn't look like a person who had retired. He looked in good shape. So to finish his career with that, you can't ask for more. At the point when the fight was over, I thought to myself, You've won it. But it's close and you're on their turf, so you don't know what to expect. But that is the thing that you can always talk about – when you even think about it you've got to smile. And I remember when Barrington got the decision: when I fought, in my fighting days, and won, I didn't go parading, I've never been like that. Even when Barrington wins a lot of times I just go, 'Yeah, well done'; you feel it inside, not externally. But when he beat Bob Schreiber, I just had to run across the ring. It was unbelievable.

The promoter promised us an amount of expenses money – they gave us 50 per cent. The tickets hadn't been cashed in because they were doing it through this ticketing machine: 'We'll sort it out when you go back tomorrow morning. Give us your bank details and we'll post it.' We are still waiting for it five years later. But if you'd have said to me, 'The *money or that win,' we'd probably have said the win. So even though I'm a bit disappointed that they promised us this money but we've never had it, I'm still happy about it. Bob Schreiber is really principled, a nice guy, really likeable and an amazing fighter. Barrington is new to that sport really. But that guy's been doing it a long time. That was a dream – actually standing in the ring with Schreiber on the other side, something I didn't think I'd see. Who could ever, on my account, end up fighting somebody like that? The great thing about the Dutch is they like a good sportsperson; they will cheer you. That's what I loved about going there.*

His cheeky wife, after I was declared the winner, came over to me and said, 'This is our country,' like she was expecting him to win on a hometown decision.

But life is all about taking a risk. Coming from here and going to somebody else's country and fighting 'em: when you see all those big boxing shows and you see those 20,000 people, you think, *I've been in that situation myself.* And when you come out and you see so many people cheering you, even in a foreign country, you just go to another planet. But even when I'd lost the fight, the Dutch were cheering for me to come back again. Because I wasn't just a fighter, I was a good showman as well.

* * *

A little while after this, I was working in a designer menswear shop. This girl walked in the shop and said, 'You're that guy off that TV programme.' I went, 'Yeah.' She was just stalking me, man! I say that to people to tease her.

TRACEY

I'll tell the true version. I worked on the doors for about 11 years and I knew a lot of Barrington's friends, though I didn't know him. I was one of the first doorwomen to work in the industry. I was training in the gym one day with my best pal Mikey, who's enormous, when this guy came in who ran some of the doors in Birmingham – he came in to pay some of the lads their money.

He said to Mikey, 'Who's that bird over there?'

'That's Tracey – we kind of box together.'

'We need some birds on the door for an opening night in Broad Street, Birmingham.'

So Mikey put it to me and I said, 'Oh I don't know – I'm a single mum, I have a six-year-old.'

'No, you'll be all right; you'll be working with some good lads.'

From the first night that club opened, I actually stayed working on the door for 11 years. I've seen it all: drunken people jumping out of hotel windows, or people held up at gunpoint. You get to a stage when you just want to get home all in one piece. I had a normal day job – I was an office manager for a security company during the day, but I was always on the door on a Friday and Saturday night.

I knew people who knew Barrington; they used to come in the club. I'd obviously heard of him and they kept showing him on Danny Dyer's show. A couple of days later, I went into the shop where he worked – I always used to go in there, it was a women's shop as well at the time. I used to buy my handbags in there and I used to say to my friends, 'They put all the attractive ones in there on the stand,' and they used to laugh because none of them found him attractive!

He was in there but we didn't speak. So when I left the shop he asked Little Baz, one of the lads who were working there, who I was. Then, a couple of weeks later, I went in the shop again and we got talking.

He always says I was stalking him! I did say, 'You're off of Danny Dyer,' that's how the conversation started.

When I left the shop he asked Little Baz for my number and we chatted – and I actually invited him out for dinner. So I said to him, 'I wanna meet you in the afternoon as you could be a mad axe-man for all I know!' Little did I know, I wasn't that far from the truth. We met in the afternoon, I took him to a nice place and I had 21 blue and white roses shipped in from Amsterdam, to give him when I met him. No one had ever really done anything for him like that on the first date.

So he's walking out to the car after the meal and I'm

like, 'I've got to go before it gets dark.' It was the first time we'd spent any time together so I just wanted to get out of there before it got dark.

We've gone out to my car and I've given him the roses; he's flummoxed; gobsmacked. He's thrown himself in the car, taken off.

He phoned me up about half an hour later: 'You invited me out to dinner and bought me flowers – things like that don't happen to me.'

After a couple of days, he always used to phone me and I never phoned him once. He was phoning me for about a week or so and one day he said to me, 'Why don't you ever phone me?' I said, 'Because if you want to speak to me you'll phone me. I don't feel the need to chase you.' I know that people like him are used to being chased and I don't do chasing.

We met for the first time in 2008 – and then, after his 2012 court case, Barrington made his marriage proposal. Still to this day, now that we're married, I don't phone him from when he leaves the house to when he comes back. I've learned. I've seen all the married doormen having three or four girls in the same club, and basically it clued me up as to what men are like. In fact, working with them clued me up far too much.

I started seeing her and here I am today. I married Tracey on Saturday, 22 September 2012; we'd been together for about four years. To be fair, she's the only woman who has never wanted anything from me and she's not with me because of my reputation – which is what I think happened in the past.

CHAPTER FOURTEEN

In Birmingham and much of Coventry, I'm still getting trailed by the police and they know I don't like them anyway. I'm a bastard to the police: if you talk to me like I'm a cunt, I'm going to talk to you back like a cunt. Half of the police know who I am and know my reputation, so they talk to me like arseholes. But sometimes now I've got to hold my tongue – I'm getting old; I'm not as fit as I used to be; I'm not a fighter like I used to be.

But still, every couple of months, I got stopped by a policeman: 'Whose car is it?'

'What do you ask me such a stupid fuckin' question for? You know it's my car – you know it's registered to me. It's not as if you don't know who I am.'

In one case, this particular officer was talking down to me. I said, 'Just give me your name and number and do what you've gotta do.' I took his name and number, and when he'd finished with me I went straight to the police station and reported his fucking arse to the superintendent for talking to me like a fucking arsehole.

I'm always going to have the police on me. Say, for instance, there's an urgent incident and the police hear my name, one car's not going to come: it's probably going to be one or two meat wagons with dogs. If I go to football, I've got to watch it: 'Barrington's 'ere, he's got about 20 guys around with him.'

There was a good firm of us a few seasons ago at Stoke. When you come off the motorway, going about two miles in towards Stoke, there's this really quiet pub where you don't get any football fans at all. We all landed there, having a drink, and one of the firm went into the car park to have a spliff. The next minute, about 20 to 40 police turned up: 'You guys will have to come out of the pub.'

We were a couple of miles away from the ground because we went offsite, hoping the police wouldn't notice where we were. But some lads were in the car park and the police had noticed it and called for reinforcements.

'We ain't causing any trouble, we're just having a drink!'

It was an out-of-town pub, like a Beefeater, where families go for dinner. But the police searched my car and I had my training kit with some nunchukas in the bag.

'What you doing with them?'

'I use them for training, mate.'

'What's your name?'

I told them that if they checked my record they'd see that I'm a Mixed Martial Arts fighter. He took the nunchukas off me and said he wasn't arresting me, but we all had to leave and they'd escort us to the football match.

There were around 15 to 20 cars with a police escort. The escort included vans, cars, bikes – everything! We went right through the traffic and we felt like royalty. Then we got into the ground and watched the match, but nothing went off. It was boring really, a bit of banter but that was it. The police wouldn't let the Blues lads out and there were a couple of them sat in the Stoke end anyway.

When we came out of the ground at the back there was a big wire mesh that separated us from Stoke fans. Some of the lads tried to climb up and pull it down, but the police were bashing everyone. Everything was going off around us but we just couldn't get out. All we could see were pockets of Blues and Stoke.

* * *

Two seasons ago, I got done by the police. My mate Scouse had just come out of prison. The Blues were playing Villa and there were about 10 of us down by the train station; I came off the train from Coventry with Rupert and met the others. Scouse was smoking a spliff outside the station. I said, 'Come on, Scouse, you can't do this shit outside anymore.' He'd been in jail for four years. Somebody walked past and smelled the spliff, then went and complained to a policeman. We were just standing there when six or seven police came walking over. 'Someone has complained about somebody smoking illegal substances, so we are gonna search you.'

'All right, search me,' I said.

I'd gone to Coventry to pick up Rupert. He was lagging so he still had his clothes on from the night before. He was getting scared now as he was carrying something, so, all of a sudden, he tried to do a runner. The police grabbed him and threw him on the floor. They started hitting him and I thought, *I can't just stand there and watch this!* So I ran over and grabbed this policeman, threw him over and pulled another one off Rupert too. Then they sprayed some gas in my face.

I went to court and got charged with assaulting police officers. I got community service and a fine for that. I didn't get a match ban though.

TODD

I know that Barrington's got a good heart and he's got a lot of love for his friends, but I think the day that it really dawned on me was when we were all going to the Blues/Villa game. I think it was a cup match, maybe a league game, but we all met up in New Street station and were just chilling. Someone turns round to me and says, 'I want to go for a fag.' I said OK, so we went outside and he lit up a joint. Soon as we'd had this joint, we moved off (we only had three drags) and the other lads moved outside to have a cigarette. So we've left them and, as we're walking to get some food, all these riot police are walking past us.

I didn't think anything of it; I just thought they were going outside. But they've gone to Rupert, 'We wanna search you,' and Rupert really wasn't into being searched. He just said, 'Well I wasn't smoking the joint, why do you wanna search me?' Then he's gone to walk away but all the police have jumped him, there must have been at least 15 of them. The police have got Rupert and it's a no-win situation, but Barrington's been with Rupert in Coventry over the years and I know how close they are, I can see the love. So Barrington's just run at the police and held his arms out as wide as he could. He went to take them all down just for Rupert and they gassed him, they were cuffing him and I was thinking, We're supposed to be having it with Villa. *They took them all down the station but, when they got there, because Barrington's so high profile, one of the police with the pips on his shoulder said, 'What's going on?' Barrington explained to him: 'I didn't like the way they were handling my mate and they've arrested me.'*

The following season, in 2010, I was walking out of the Villa/Blues match towards Digbeth. I was in the box that day and, as I left, I rang the lads to see where they were.

I came out and all the Blues were stood there chanting shit at the Villa. I thought I'd stand there and have a little singsong with the boys and, before you knew it, I was on the front line. The police were shouting, 'Move back, move back!' I turned around to move and they started bashing me with their telescopic truncheons!

I thought, *What the fuck's going on 'ere?* and I kicked a fucking policeman.

RUPERT & TODD

Todd: *Because we were meeting Barrington, we were between the police line and the rest of the Blues. They were all arguing with the police and chucking stuff; we were in the middle but we were walking up to the car. We went in a shop; when we came out, the police came up to us and tried to push us up the road and into the other Blues. We were like, 'Fuck off!' basically. But one of them came at Barrington one time too many, with a dog as well, so me and Rupert sort of backed away. The dog didn't seem to bother him as he was too busy, but the next thing is they've pushed him and Barrington's pushed back. Then they were on him like flies.*

Rupert: *They basically dragged him round by the police vans so that no one could see what was going on.*

Todd: *I got a bit of footage that we gave to his solicitors but I don't know what good it ended up doing, because there were all these police cars and vans screening it anyway and Barrington was down on the floor.*

I rang Rupert to check where they were and he said they were down by the island at The Watering Hole. I had to take him back to Coventry so I walked down there as Rupert and that lot were coming out of the pub. I said, 'Come on, Rupert, let's get the fuck out of 'ere.' I was walking along, talking on my phone, when the next minute this policeman comes walking over with a police dog and says, 'Move!'

'All right, mate! I'm going!'

We were outside a West Indian fruit shop. This other policeman came sprinting across the road with a shield and *BANG!* 'You ain't on *Deadliest Men* now, are ya?' He spanked me right in the mouth with the shield.

I said, 'Fuck you, ya cunt!'

So I've stood there in a fighting stance and I don't know where all these police came from, they just jumped on me. They started kicking me, punching me, whacking me with truncheons. All the men have surrounded me and then all the wagons have come round, so obviously nobody can get it on their mobile phones.

The first copper jumped on me and clattered me to fuck. I've had some fights in my time but this time I was fucking scared – I couldn't just curl up in a ball. They put the handcuffs on one hand but I couldn't move the other one. There were about four fucking guys on me and I'd landed on my front. 'Get your fucking hand out!' they shouted.

They're all on top of me and I'm on my back. One of

them is trying to shove a fucking truncheon up my arse and I'm shouting, '*Ahhhhh!*'

Then they picked me up and threw me in the van, shouting, 'Fucking Zulu nigger!'

'Yeah, fuck you! I shagged your missus last night.'

I thought I was going to get a clout in the mouth, as I was calling them fat bastards and all that. The worst thing of all was there was a black officer in the meat wagon. I turned around to this nigger and said, 'Oi, you fucking coconut! You're just sitting there while they crack all these nigger jokes!' He just turned around and looked the opposite way. Obviously he wouldn't say a thing or he'd look out of place.

It was about an hour till they took me to the police station. I got in front of the sergeant and he told me to empty my pockets. 'I'm gonna have to search you now.' Then he grabbed hold of my bollocks! So I grabbed him and threw him against the fucking wall.

'Barrington, calm down, this is all on camera!' said one of my four mates that they'd arrested, trying to cool it down.

'I've just been kicked in the fucking bollocks, he's tried grabbing my balls and that cunt was trying to ram the fucking truncheon up my arse!'

They arrested me and put me in a cell. The sergeant wasn't that meaty, he was a fucking prick; he was probably in the army and got bullied, or the type of person who got bullied at school.

A couple of hours later, I started coughing and blood was coming up. I couldn't go to the toilet until 8.30am the next morning, but I had pains in my stomach and was vomiting blood – so I rang the buzzer. The doctor came to see me and I got about a day and a half in the hospital. I had a catheter put up my fucking dick because I couldn't piss.

I came out the next day and went to Lloyd's House, the police headquarters. I tried to put in a complaint but they told me they couldn't deal with it until the case had come to court. So, at the court case, I was told I was banned from any match until the case had finished – it went on for months and months. A year and a half later, the case went to crown court. The worst thing is that the police knew, from two previous crown court appearances, that they never had anything on me. They had nothing from day fucking one!

The police said in court, 'He was in a fighting stance and he was fighting us.'

I knew damn well that, when the police went to a high-profile match like the Blues/Villa game, a lot of them had little handheld camcorders. So, if I'm fighting police rather than defending myself – come on, there has to be someone there with a video of it. Where's the evidence that I was fighting the police? There was no evidence at all. There were six policemen and no independent witnesses, and it didn't even go to the day. My barrister got together with their prosecutor and said,

'You've got nothing on him and you're going to have to give up the charge.'

I turned around to the policeman in charge on the spot: 'Fuck you, you cunt! Better luck next time.'

And a couple of weeks later, I went down to police headquarters – because now I wanted to press charges against all these fucking policemen. They didn't want to fucking know!

* * *

Coventry played Millwall a couple of seasons ago and I thought, *I want to go to this match!* I went down there with about 10 guys; we're having it off, but by the time I look round everyone's run off. Just like when Coventry played Villa: I went down there, had it off outside with the Villa firm – and then they've all run off and left me.

But, in September 2011, a firm of us flew to Croatia for the Maribor (Slovenia) v Birmingham City game. We hired a car and me and my good pal Terry spent a night in Croatia before crossing the border for the Maribor game. Now it's no secret that they can be a racist firm. Everywhere I went I was getting stared at; their Old Bill were growling at me.

To be fair though, we did take over the place.

We won the game so we were well pleased. Terry had been talking on the Internet for a while with the top geezer from the Dynamo Zagreb firm, Bad Blue Boys;

they invited us to go and watch a game on their turf. I was well up for a bit of that but my pal was a bit more cautious. We met up with them though after the Maribor game, when we drove back into Zagreb and were treated like kings: VIP treatment in their nightclub, it was proper.

It was also full of racists. I was only the second black guy ever to set foot on their terraces. (The other guy wasn't invited so he got bashed.) There were thousands of white heads and my black head in the middle of them. It was funny; they were a cracking bunch of lads and I still keep in contact with them.

CHAPTER
FIFTEEN

About a year after the police jumped me outside the Blues/Villa game, this guy I'd known for about 30-odd years came over and said to me, 'Baz, I've had a grow [some cannabis plants] go missing. I reckon the guy down the shop has robbed it. I went down the shop about two days beforehand and there's about three big heavies there. Please go down with me just in case the lumps are there. I need to talk with this guy.'

So I said, 'All right then, no problem.' He asked me to come down and show a bit of face because I'm a well-known guy – OK, I agreed. I've known this guy for 30-odd years – I didn't care because he *used to be* one of my close friends.

It had been going on for about two or three days already, so I arranged the meeting down this shop in

Quinton, Birmingham. On the day, I went to the shop, and as I turned round the corner he was standing there with about four or five other guys. So I said to him, 'I thought it was just me and you going down to see the guy?'

'Oh, I've just brought some other guys to stand on in case anything happens.'

OK, fuck it, I'll just carry on. I went, 'All right, fair enough, no problem.'

In my mind, I'm prepared to have it off anyway – no matter what situation I'm going into. I've been in those situations before – I'm there to have it. But I didn't go down with tools or anything, thinking there was going to be big trouble. If a mate asked me to go and do anything, I'd do it – I don't ask questions.

So I let them walk in front of me and, all of a sudden, my mobile phone rang. I was on the phone but they carried on; I saw them walking to the shop but I stayed on my phone. I ended the call and, after about 30 seconds, I walked to the shop.

As I opened the door, it was all kicking off: the other guys had this geezer by the counter and were beating the shit out of him with their fists. So I thought, *Fuck this, I'm out of 'ere!* I've looked around and walked straight out of the shop, jumped into my car and done one.

Then, a couple of days later, just before Prince Wills and Wossname got married on 29 April 2011, my solicitor rang me and said, 'The police down Bournville station want to talk to you.' Straight away I knew what they wanted to talk to me about.

So I arranged to go up to the police station on the day the royalty were getting married. I turned up there with a solicitor and they said, 'You're under arrest for suspicion of blackmail and two assault charges.'

'What the fuck are you on about, blackmail and two assault charges? I ain't assaulted no one! I ain't demanded anything off no one!'

'You threatened this man and hit him with a knuckle-duster.'

'I ain't got a clue what you're on about, mate.'

This lad's reading me what's supposed to have happened: they're demanding 40-odd thousand pounds off this geezer; apparently £5000 was dropped in a bin at McDonald's near Birmingham City's ground; apparently some guy's gone to the bin to pick the money up and then got arrested.

So I got arrested. My brief said I was looking at five years. I just went, 'No comment – no comment – no comment' in my interview. They didn't let me out. They kept me in overnight, took me to court on the Monday and I got bail. After everything, I kept thinking, *There's no way I'm pleading guilty to something I haven't done.*

I'd had runback off my so-called mate: 'This is what you've gotta say, this is what you've gotta say!'

'Oh fuck you! You've put me in this position now; I'm not gonna get five years for something I haven't done!'

But now, because of my new missus, who's well clued up on things like that, we've been reading all the statements I've got from the barrister. This guy down the shop said he knows me from the clubs downtown: I've never set eyes on the guy in my life. He's said I'm a cage fighter: obviously he's seen me on the fucking TV. I don't know this guy from Adam. In his statement, he said I hit him with a knuckleduster and I forced his son to lie on the ground.

Come on, I was a professional fighter! If I hit you with a knuckleduster, you wouldn't know what fucking time of day it was!

So after these guys were in the shop beating them, when the police came to the shop, he said, 'I'd just had an argument with the guys because I'd sold this guy some dodgy equipment,' and then the police left; he didn't want to press charges. But then two weeks later he did. He apparently explained to the police that these guys had been demanding 40-odd grand off him; they said if you don't pay the money we're going to do this to you, we're going to do that to you, which had nothing to do with me.

When I was arrested, the police were going through the statements: they had no telephone records of me having any contact with anybody else except for three telephone calls with my ex-mate – and that was the odd time that he was saying to me, 'Hey look, I want you to come down the shop with me.' But between him, the guy who's got the shop and another couple of guys, all the telephone conversations tied up with the whole lot of them.

So I knew they didn't have anything on me. The guy picked me out of the ID parade: I held my hand up and said, 'Yeah, I was there! I didn't go down there for no trouble, I just went down there with my pal and when it all happened I just turned round and walked out.'

Of course, when all this happened, the police didn't want to know about it until they heard my name. It's the same as when I got arrested for the football a couple of years before; the same guy arrested me again.

I was on bail for eight or nine months before I went to Birmingham Crown Court: the trial lasted about two weeks in April 2012. I don't know whether this is a record or not, but we went through five sets of jurors in this case. Because on the first day of my trial they called in the jurors and one of them sent a note to the judge, saying that they knew me. Every time the jury came out, somebody knew me or knew one of the other defendants. I think it got to the stage where they were going to put the case out to another court, but, wherever I am, I know so many people – or so many people know me. This went on all day. After five later attempts, we still couldn't start the trial

I think they were getting sick and tired of having to keep swearing in juries all the time. On the sixth attempt, we got a jury; they eventually managed to find jurors who didn't know anyone. Deep down I knew I was going to get out of it because I'd been in the wrong place at the wrong time.

On the first day of my trial, I didn't take my missus to court as there are just some places you don't take her. The prosecution looked moody, as always, but that was a minor point as I had a good barrister.

Before the trial started, I got all the depositions from my brief. To be honest, I didn't have a clue what I was looking for, but Tracey spent hours going over them. She never stopped; she turned into a brief overnight. She requested transcripts of the only 999 call that was made plus copies of the alleged victim's son's statement, as he was in the shop on the day. If he saw his dad get beaten up and he made a police statement, why wasn't he being used as a witness?

She got all this info from my barrister and spent hours going over it. It transpired that the victim's son had said in his statement that I was the last to arrive at the shop and I didn't hit anyone. In fact, I stepped in when someone went to hit the guy's son – hence why he wasn't being used as a witness, and why the statement was missing from the original court documents.

So far that's one-nil to me.

Now to the guy who made the 999 call: during the call he states there are 10 men going into a shop; I am parked over the road at the junction, watching them fighting in the shop. He clearly states that no weapons were seen; when asked by the operator, 'Do you know these men?'

he states, 'I don't know them, never seen them before.' He then gives his name and ends the call.

The next day, Tracey went up to the shop and parked where the alleged witness did. There is a 20-foot drop from the dual carriageway down to where the shop is; you can't see the front of the shop as there is a 20-foot concrete advertising board. She had to go right up to the window to look in and got loads of photos that would later prove this guy wasn't where he said he was. I always said he was in the back and didn't want to explain what he was doing in a shop that sells crop equipment.

That's two-nil to me.

As the guy left his name on the 999 call, Tracey looked him up and did a background check on him. I couldn't believe it when she showed me what she found: he was due in court for cultivating cannabis to the value of £20,000. Bingo, caught out again!

We couldn't find his police statement in the court papers but we found a statement from a guy with a different name, referring to the 999 call that was made. That statement was made six months later, in which he goes on to name me and my two co-accused and states we were carrying bats and had hoods on. Unbelievable!

Where the fuck had this guy come from?

Tracey did a background check on him and he had no criminal history. He didn't even exist on any public records. But it transpired that the guy who made the 999 call with the long criminal history had been given a new name and a clean record to give evidence against us. So that's three-nil to me.

The next day at court, Tracey gave all the information to the barrister and he wasn't happy. He went straight into the prosecution and kicked off with them for trying to pull a flanker. The prosecution decided not to call their only witness, so that left the alleged victim.

When the 'victim' got in the witness box, he told the funniest stories of how he was attacked by at least 10 people using bats and knuckledusters, and how he remained standing through the whole thing. We were in the dock pissing ourselves laughing. So were the jury – his medical records showed a four-centimetre scratch on his lip. Even the judge cracked a smile.

When my barrister was questioning the 'victim', he said, 'What kind of things do you sell in your shop?'

'I sell equipment to grow indoor plants like tomatoes.' That one had the court in fits again. What a twat!

'So you don't condone people growing cannabis then?'

'Oh no. I've never had anything to do with drugs. I run a legitimate business.'

This guy was saying that, although he's got a grow shop, he's got nothing to do with any grow, but my missus caught him out. When we got home from court that day, Tracey still wasn't giving up. She got back on the computer, set up a blag email address and asked the guy at the shop for advice on a crop. Of course, he's got a webpage: 'Buy this! Dust for buds,' and things like that.

So she sent him an email: 'I've got some little buds, I want to get my buds bigger. What do I do?' He sent her an email back: 'There isn't anything you can tell me about crops. I've done loads. I can sell you this fan and that chemical to get your crop sorted.'

What a mug!

So then we printed it off and gave it to our barrister the next day, and he gave it to the prosecution. When the 'victim' was in the witness box behind his screen, my barrister waved the email at him and read it out to the jury. He was wounded. What could he say? I would have loved to see his face.

Even the judge looked over at my missus and gave her a sly smile.

It's now four-nil to me but, as we know, you haven't won till the final whistle goes.

I was next in the witness box. My barrister had the whole court in fits of laughter; he did me proud that day. He said, 'Hold up your fist, Mr Patterson,' then he turned and looked at the jury and said, 'Do you think Mr Patterson needs to use a knuckleduster, even if they do make them to fit hands the size of an elephant's foot? If Mr Patterson hit the victim with a bare hand, we could safely say he would still be lying down.'

He then went on to wave my book contract around and asked, 'Do you think Mr Patterson has to resort to blackmail when he has a lucrative book deal and parts in films? We have all seen how well known Mr Patterson is;

it's taken six juries to get this trial underway, so why would he roll up in a convertible with the roof off and no disguise to beat up the alleged victim?'

The jury was out. There was nothing else anyone could do now but sit and wait. No matter how well it had all gone, you can never be sure until you hear the foreman of the jury say those words: 'guilty' or 'not guilty'.

We went for a walk and came back; they were still out. At 4.30pm, we were sent home till the next morning; at 2.00pm that day, our barrister called us: 'The jury are back.'

As they all walked back into court, none of them looked over at me or my co-accused. That's never a good sign.

The judge said, 'Have you reached a verdict on all three of the defendants?'

'No, your honour.'

'Who have you reached a verdict on?'

'Mr Patterson.'

I'm now thinking they're going to make an example out of me.

'What is your verdict?'

'Not guilty on all counts.'

I was buzzing. It was finally all over. This case had been hanging over me for a year.

The jury were sent away to battle it out over my two co-accused. One of my pals had brought in his jail bag just in case. Not me – I don't do that. It's bad luck.

When the jury came back on my two pals, the judge said he would accept a majority verdict. They both got a 'not guilty' on a ten to two. What a result!

When the case started, it was front-page news: 'Barrington Patterson in blackmail plot'. I got a 'not guilty' and it was two lines on page six. Jokers!

After the trial, I asked my missus to marry me. To my surprise, she said yes. In 12 weeks, she got the whole thing sorted: she had the dress made and got me and my best man, Todd, suited and booted, with a lavish reception for all our friends and family.

Just days before the wedding, I got a call from the manager of the venue saying the Old Bill had been to see him. They were concerned that we were having our wedding reception there, as the Blues were playing less than a mile away that day against Reading. But who the fuck are Reading?

I'm not telling my missus about the call. I need to think about this one. Then she calls me, having a fit. She's copped wind of it and she's going mad; she calls up the copper to sort it out and they want to put Old Bill outside the reception. She tells them it isn't happening and that she isn't organising her wedding around the football fixtures. So it all went ahead without the Old Bill.

It was a wicked day! There were 400 people there in all. It was nice for all of us to be in the same place for a happy occasion – the only time we get together on that scale is for funerals. Loads of people have since asked: 'Can't we have another party like that one?'

* * *

Sometimes I thrive on the little bit of reputation I've got, it's nice and all that. I went up to Whitley Bay on my birthday for a stag night: 'Hello, Barrington, how you doin', mate? You wanna drink?' 'If you wanna buy us a drink, buy us a drink.' 'You're that bloke off the telly, aren't ya?' 'Yeah – buy us a drink.' So sometimes it's a good thing and sometimes it goes the opposite way.

I look ahead but I don't plan things – I just live from day to day. The reason is that before my dad died he planned a lot of things: he planned to retire; apparently, he was going on holiday with his wife when he retired. He never got to his retirement; he died a couple of weeks before.

Once he was older and about to stop working, I'd go down and see my dad at Wisbech, whereas my other brother and sisters wouldn't. Colleen will say, 'Your dad wanted you to have this' – they don't mention my brother and sisters, it's like they don't exist. He's got a daughter in New York and they don't mention her at all.

But when I go down there Colleen gives me things – 'Here's £1000 towards the wedding, your dad would have wanted you to have it.' I sat her on the top table at my wedding.

My dad passed away in January 2006 of cancer. Up until

then he was as fit as a fiddle, working and living a quiet life with Colleen near Peterborough. I will always be grateful that he saw me fight professionally. When he passed away I grieved for him – but I also grieved for the lost years.

ANDRE

Barrington has got a heart of gold and a soft side to him that not many people have seen, barring his close friends and family. I have seen Barrington at his lowest points, like when his dad died and we went together to the funeral in Norfolk. This hit Baz really hard but, like brothers, you stick together through the hard times to help each other through it. Baz always comes and talks to me when he has a problem and I do the same with him. Or else Baz just takes the piss to make you laugh when you're down.

Barrington is so soft with his children – if you could see him around them it's not 'Big Bad Baz'; he just melts, but that's the nice side of him that people don't see.

I was honoured to be godfather to his son Kye, and Barrington was best man at my wedding to my beautiful wife, Alana, and did us proud on the day. Once again, the soft side of Baz came out in the words he wrote about me and Alana. Top man!

Barrington has finally settled down and I know that he loves his new bride, Tracey, dearly. I wish them all the best for the future.

From his brother, Andre Yerou

So as for me, I don't plan a thing. I take each day as it comes. You plan things, they never work out. I get up in the morning, thank God I'm alive; I go to bed, thank God and ask him to make sure I wake up in the morning.

I just live my life; I try to treat each day as if it's my last day on earth. So I'm glad to enjoy each day as it comes. If I had my time all over again I wouldn't change anything.